Mothers Talk About
Learning Disabilities

Books by Elizabeth Weiss

The Anger Trap

Recovering from the Heart Attack Experience

From Female Depression to Contented Womanhood

Female Fatigue

The Female Breast

ELIZABETH WEISS

Mothers Talk About Learning Disabilities

Personal Feelings, Practical Advice

PRENTICE
HALL
PRESS

New York   London   Toronto   Sydney   Tokyo

Author's Note

The mothers and children described in this book are real. To preserve their privacy, their names, ages, and identities have been changed. Some selections represent composites of several children. However, the experts in the field, interviewed for their professional opinions, have been identified accurately.

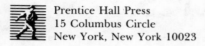

Prentice Hall Press
15 Columbus Circle
New York, New York 10023

Copyright © 1989 by Elizabeth Weiss

PRENTICE HALL PRESS and colophon are registered trademarks of Simon & Schuster, Inc.

Library of Congress Cataloging-in-Publication Data

Weiss, Elizabeth S.
   Mothers talk about learning disabilities: personal feelings,
practical advice / Elizabeth Weiss.—1st Prentice Hall Press ed.
     p. cm.
   Includes index.
   ISBN 0-13-602970-1
   1. Learning disabled children—United States. 2. Learning
disabled children—United States—Family relationships. 3. Mothers—
United States—Psychology. I. Title.
LC4705.W45 1989
306.8'74—dc19   89-3845
                                         CIP

Manufactured in the U.S.A.

10 9 8 7 6 5 4 3 2 1

First Edition

To my sons, Mark and Greg,
of whom I am proud beyond any words,
and to my husband, Stan,
whose steadiness anchored us all

Acknowledgments

One mother's story offers a unique perspective. The thoughts, feelings, and experiences of scores of mothers create a universality of much deeper meaning. I am greatly indebted to the many women who openly and honestly shared their stories with me. Out of respect for their personal and family privacy, I have not listed their names. This, in no way, diminishes my thanks and gratitude.

Growing up is a complex journey: The confidence, motivation, and skills instilled by educators, teachers, and friends can greatly affect the road taken. I would like to thank the following individuals who made a real difference for my children: Roanna Shorofsky, Elaine Schwebel, Andrea Kaminsky, Eddie Locke, Yvette Siegel, Peter Mertens, and Selma Affatey.

Mothers Talk About Learning Disabilities brings the experiences of real mothers and real children to many more mothers and children, bonding us in strength. While this spirit was inspiring, like all books, this one was possible only through diligent effort. For their hard work and belief in this project, I am grateful to my typist, Vera Morangello, who willingly typed and retyped; my agent, Carol Abel, who said those wonderful words, "I love your book"; Lyn Hogan, an editorial assistant who looked beyond the usual professional manifestoes and found meaning in a mother's message; and my editor, Gail Winston, who caringly shepherded the manuscript through all the necessary stages to produce this attractive book.

Last, but foremost in my thoughts, I want to thank my husband,

Stan, who was always there, keeping our family sail steady and facing forward. I am truly happy to see him walk in the door each evening. And, of course, a thank-you hug for Mark and Greg. Far too often children with learning disabilities are pictured as misfits, or, as Greg would say, "Geek of the Week." It is my hope that my children and the many terrific children pictured in these pages will dispel this unfair perception.

Contents

INTRODUCTION

Why I Wrote This Book

I wrote this book for me. I am the mother of two boys: Mark is now fourteen and Greg is twelve. When I discovered that my children had learning problems, they were still very young. At the time, more than anything else, I wanted to speak with other mothers. I felt such hurt and confusion—indeed, such a jumble of strong emotions—that I desperately wanted to hear from other mothers who had children with similar problems. I yearned for their words of advice and understanding. However, I did not know any.

As a writer, my next thought was to go to the library. There I found shelves and shelves of books by educators and professionals. The things they recommended for a parent to do seemed endless. While technical jargon and advice on manipulatives abounded, I could not find a single book by a mother. I wanted to hear from mothers because I felt that only another mother could really understand what I was feeling. I wanted to know if, in fact, my feelings were abnormal, excessive, or out-of-line. I wanted to know if other women found their relations with their husbands suddenly under strain, as I did. I wanted to know if the problems seemed to pervade their homes, as they did my home. I wanted to help myself cope with the day-to-day frustrations, and I wanted to get myself to a place where I felt less ambivalent and less in conflict about my proper expectations for my children, as well as myself.

So, it is out of my own turmoil and uncertainty that this book was born. Writing it, however, was far from a simple decision to make. Foremost, I was fearful it would hurt my children. I wanted to make things better and lessen stress—not increase it. I also did not want to reveal too much of our private lives because I feared this might cause more harm than good. I did not want my children to read the book as they got older and misinterpret, or misunderstand, my statements and feelings.

I also hesitated because every time I began to write I experienced severe writer's block. Recently, we visited the La Brea tar pits in Los Angeles, where prehistoric animals got stuck in deep pools of tar. At the museum, children can pull levers up and down to see how difficult it was for the animals to move in this tar. My writing seemed much like that—slow, laborious, and difficult.

On previous books, I had approached my material with confidence and clarity. Yet, on this topic, where I unquestionably had so much first-hand knowledge and experience, I found myself tentative and unsure. Without doubt, this was because solutions with my own children had been neither clear nor easy. Indeed, what had worked one year often did not work the next, what had worked like a charm for one child did not seem to be right at all for the other. I did not really have any "how-to" advice for other mothers. I had not found "the answer." Was it worth writing if I could offer no solutions?

Although I had no magic answers, I was convinced that what I had experienced and what other mothers were thinking, feeling, and doing was vitally important. Over and over psychologists tell us of the pivotal role of a mother in a child's life. Therefore, I believed that the role of "special" mothers, although overlooked, was significant and deserved my study and effort.

So this book is about and for mothers. I felt, however, that the views of professionals in the field could not be ignored. By explaining causes, compensatory strategies, and parenting approaches, I believed their suggestions and insights would be helpful to mothers.

Of course, there could be no mother's book at all were it not for the one thing that links us all—our children. Very early, I noticed that my own children were acutely aware of the feelings of others; many of their friends shared this gentle sensitivity. The thoughts and feelings of these children form a crucial and moving part of this story.

When I was first told of our children's learning disabilities, I was concerned about what the future might hold for them. Thinking of the sophisticated demands and complexities of modern life, I was worried what such a diagnosis might mean. Now, ten years later, I am much more optimistic and positive. I see their future as exceedingly bright.

At the beginning, I was very impatient, wanting my children to read sooner, spell better, speak more articulately, and catch a ball faster. I was ambivalent about supportive services, wishing they did not need them, and wanting those they did have to work faster. Now, ten years later, I see that these services did make a difference but, most important, my children learned on their time-table, not mine. The struggle was not always easy for them or me. But I am proud, beyond any words, of them.

Both my sons are now in regular school. Yes, I still see too many quiz scores of 64, 49, and 51. Yes, I still hear too many teachers' comments that they are easily distracted and inattentive, and that they must be more careful to take good class notes and to take more time studying these notes at home. Yes, organization is still difficult and foreign language is extremely tough. But this year, Mark was elected president of his class and made the varsity tennis team (the only middle school student to make the team). Greg is outgoing and popular. Whereas he once had difficulty catching a ball, he is now an ace first baseman who plays with a skill that would make even his idol, Mets star Keith Hernandez, proud. He also plays the drums with an ability that amazes me.

More significant to me than any specific achievement, however, I am thrilled with them—their smiles, their joy, and their enthusiasm for life. They are terrific charming kids: wonderful, caring, funny, and good people. So it is this message of hope I want to send to those mothers first struggling with learning problems.

1

I Have an LD Child

No educational therapist, no teacher, not even a psychiatrist can know how it feels to have a child with learning problems. Only a mother knows.

My first response upon learning that my older son had a learning disability was not to tell anyone. It felt like a deep hurt, almost a physical wound that, if touched even slightly, would bleed and hurt. While I ached for him, the first hurt was my own. It seemed a condemnation of me, like a secret that somehow had been revealed. All my worst feelings about myself came rushing to the surface.

Long-forgotten childhood hurts came to mind with an intensity that deeply disturbed me. I remembered standing in line before my high school final exams almost panicked by all the facts I had to remember. I recalled sitting in math class and finding the word problems (those trains forever going in the opposite directions) utterly baffling. I had absolutely no idea where to begin. My mind flashed back to my father sitting with me, night after night, going over the multiplication tables. He was endlessly patient and encouraging, but I remembered that confused feeling inside. I certainly did not want that for my child.

While I never did poorly in school—indeed, I achieved in the upper quarter of my class—I still began to wonder if I had had learning disabilities. My parents, friends, and husband told me this was not the case, but I still found it hard to separate myself from my child.

Not only was I reminded of painful times, I also felt so ill-suited for the task. It reminded me of climbing a steep difficult mountain. One needed to be surefooted. How could I ever carry my two children up the mountainside? It did not seem possible. They needed someone steady and patient; I was quick and impatient. They needed someone methodical; I had always been disorganized. It just seemed like a terrible match. I felt I did not have the strength or the skill.

This book is the story of my climb. It is also the story of scores of other mothers across our country. I wanted to talk with other mothers because I wanted to know what was really going on behind the closed doors of their homes and, more privately, in their hearts. I wished to know their honest feelings, stripped of the veil of societal propriety, competition, and secrecy that separates us in our daily lives.

While the women I spoke with represented very different ages and backgrounds, I found their emotional feelings and deep desire to help their children remarkably similar. Because no retelling can capture the full force and power of real experiences, here are some of their stories, as they told them.

• ▪ •

Jane and her husband, Bill, have four children. Evan, age nine, is their third child. They live in Los Angeles, where Evan attends a special school.

"I think the anticipation of the future is the hardest part for me. I can handle the day-to-day problems now, but the unknowingness of the next ten years really bothers me. If someone could say, 'he'll be a happy adult; he'll be happy, satisfied, self-sufficient,' then I could relax. But now, I don't feel I should let anything slide. It causes big conflicts.

"I want him to work every minute. Sure I know this is not possible, but I think of all he must learn, and I just don't know. I am constantly struggling, constantly trying to balance his potential and my expectations. I don't want him to feel guilty, unhappy, or disappointed in himself. Yet, he must do certain tasks—get through school, hopefully graduate, hopefully college. It goes on and on.

"With the other children, I'm confident of their abilities. I do not worry deeply if they do not do something. But with Evan, I am always worried, concerned, and then I feel guilty about all I am imposing. There is always conflict about what he can and can't do. So much is unpredictable. I know I have to be understanding of limitations. It's easy to say, but not so easy or clear in everyday life.

"He seems as happy as his siblings, but from my perspective their life is so much easier. He doesn't have their ease in doing things and, naturally, this is reflected in his attitude. He has many more anxieties, fears.

"Lots of times, I feel things are almost overwhelming, out of my control. But you cope because you have absolutely no choice. Sure, I'd change things if I could, but I can't. I must cope. Often I get angry at myself for not being more patient, more helpful, more able to solve it. I think every parent feels that way.

"For me, there is a certain anger. Why me? Why him? My life would be very different if he did not have these problems. Sometimes I feel anger that my nice, easy, fun life was somehow taken from me. But we are a strong family unit. We help each other. The kids are close. They always include him, but they are still young; sometimes I wonder what it will be like as they get older.

"I think a learning-disabled child has a powerful impact on the marriage and the whole family structure. From my experience, there are unquestionably more pulls; this will either strengthen or destroy the unit, no question about it.

"When Evan started special school, in nursery, there were seven other families. Now, it's six years later, and I think all seven marriages are no longer together.

"With Evan, it always seems something invisible is in the way of our communicating. When I am with my other children, this invisible shield does not exist. It is hard to describe, but our talking just does not flow easily. There is something 'there' always in the way.

"There are, however, certain very positive qualities that come from struggling. He's more sensitive than his brothers. They are involved with their lives, their soccer game. They take life for granted. He is much more caring, much more concerned about people. Before Evan, I just assumed my life and my children would be just like I dreamed. Now, I know life is more complex."

•　■　•

Georgina and her husband, Harry, an accountant, have one child, now a high-school senior, who was diagnosed at age three with learning disabilities. With the help of tutors, he has always been in a regular school.

"To me, my son's problems were stressful. I bet every mother will tell you the same. Mothers are the ones who bear the burden of these problems. It's tough for the fathers—very tough—but it is the mother who is on the firing line each day.

"I don't understand all the scientific explanations, but I can tell you it affects the child's total behavior. Because it pervades all areas of the child's life, it affects all areas of the mother's life. No question about it, it's a problem that's across-the-board.

"Problems get more intense when the child is under pressure. We found that whenever we tried to help our son with tutoring, language therapy, or organizational skills, it placed him under pressure, so we felt caught in a catch-22.

"I found that the only way to cope was to, at all costs, maintain a positive attitude . . . just to say to myself, 'Things are generally going in the right direction.'

"I think it's the mother's attitude that affects how she copes. I am a more optimistic person, less judgmental than my husband. I never had academic difficulties, so it is not personally threatening. My husband had many difficulties. He finds he is now reliving what he went through, and he finds it very upsetting.

"This is not to say I have always found it easy or that I can always remain calm. One of the worst times was when other children came over. It never went the way I wanted. Things were never smooth. Our son had a very short attention span. He'd lose interest before the other child got to finish. In the middle of the game he'd say he didn't want to play anymore. They would end up arguing. I had to be around. Regardless of what I did, though, it would end up in chaos. If he was with a wild child, he would become even wilder. His behavior would completely disintegrate. I encouraged him to play with children who were more mature, but they did not always want to come over.

"As he has gotten older, he has outgrown many of these social problems.

"One of the things I'm still working on is his grammar. This 'costed twenty dollars,' he will say. There is no such word as *costed,* I tell him over and over. Many times I get discouraged and feel it is futile, but somehow I keep on correcting him and he keeps on speaking poorly.

"It has certainly brought stress into our marriage. We have both reacted so differently. My husband always gets upset. 'How will he get into a good college?' he'll ask me. 'He'll end up fine. He will get there,' I always say. Sometimes I really believe it, but honestly there are times when I really do wonder.

"I think the reason the problems were not worse is because we went to a psychiatrist. He was key to us. He told us the appropriate way to do things. He was reasonable and optimistic. Frankly, I feel he made all the difference.

"I remember once we told him the only thing our son would do for an extended period is watch TV. He told us to let him do it. He explained if he enjoys it, it's alright. He needs the break. This reduced our impatience with our son's behavior and really made us a lot more relaxed.

"Our son is graduating from high school this year and now, at last, I feel that it's all coming together. The problems have not disappeared; he still has them but he has learned to compensate.

"For me, the secret has been that he was born into the right family. He was always appreciated. Even when he had all his problems—his hyperactivity, his difficulties with written expression—he was made to feel that, basically, he was terrific. Of course, I totally believed it. To me, he seemed extremely bright and I thought his disadvantages would someday become advantages. His high activity level would give him more energy for life and this has happened. His energies have become directed into scuba diving and local politics. He's able to work longer and harder than others. He is succeeding because he believes in himself and always has."

• ▪ •

Jacelyn's only child, a daughter now fourteen, has learning disabilities. She attended a special school for five years, and now goes to a private high school. Jacelyn is married and works in retailing.

"I wanted my child to be brilliant and popular, go to the best schools, and not have that feeling that she might not succeed. I wanted her to feel secure. Because I also had a difficult time in school, discovering her problem was very painful for me.

"As she has gotten older, though, things have definitely improved. I have some friends who say, 'Just wait until she's a teenager,' but I think it's the reverse. I can reason more with her now.

"When my daughter was in special school and people would ask 'Where does your child go to school?' it was awkward and, to be honest, hurtful. I don't like to say 'disability.' She doesn't have an arm or leg missing. It's not visual. Jessica is charming—she always had charm about her.

"I always felt inferior in school. I was never kept back, but I feared I would be. I was in the slow class. In junior high, we had twenty classes. It was common knowledge that the higher the number, the easier the work. I was in class twenty. To this day, I have two close friends from class twenty. They're both married to successful lawyers and have their own very interesting careers. But I still remember that frightened and empty feeling that I would get inside—that awful feeling I was going to fail. Sometimes I still feel that way. I remember when I had to speak in front of the class I would sometimes think to myself 'I really fooled you' when I did well.

"With my friends, your child is your product. I had to face that head on. I was angry when I saw certain traits in Jessica. I'm not quite as angry now. It's a problem that has to be worked on. My husband is not as critical. 'She will be fine. School is not that important,' he always says. When I look at him, I know he's right; he's extremely successful, and he was never a great student.

"In my case, I think my mother made a real difference. When I was little, she took me to ballet school. I was great at executing the movements, but I was always afraid I'd forget the combinations. My first response to anything new was 'I can't, I can't,' because keeping it all straight in my mind was so hard. When my ballet teacher asked me to demonstrate, I always performed well, but I also had to work three times as hard as the other students.

"Ballet has been immensely important to me. I stayed with it. Because it was an area where I excelled, it gave me confidence; for over fifteen years, it also gave me a career. I taught jazz exercise and I loved it. Most of all, I want to find an interest for my daughter. I really think it's key.

"I discovered she had difficulties when she was two. I'd get together with my friends and their babies. They'd have busy boxes. The children would sit and press the buttons. She'd just look at the toy; she would never even try it. My friends' children would catch on right away. Immediately, I noticed that she was different.

"In the early years, I cried almost every night. 'Why can't she be like everyone else?' I thought over and over. It was doing terrible things to me. But I got over the fact that it's not me, it's her. If she has to go to a special school, well, that's it. In the beginning, I wanted her in regular school. But I had one friend who told me sternly, "You have to do what's best for your child—not what will make you look good." It struck home.

"She acted so frustrated, both at home and at school. She was wild at home. She'd run from room to room. She'd never listen. I'd write in a diary to keep myself from hitting her, or I'd call a friend. Most friends were not very receptive. 'If your child needs special education, your child has horns' was the attitude. But some listened. It helped.

"When she was young, people would tell me, 'It gets better,' but I never honestly believed it. My child has more serious problems, I thought—they just don't understand. Now I see things do get better. It definitely takes time. You do work through it; the child matures and is better able to apply herself.

"My daughter still does not like to make mistakes, but I tell her they're only mistakes. We all make them; we can even laugh at them. I tell her I have some of the same problems because she's better off knowing.

"These days, I am much more optimistic. She's very interested in acting, and I look at her and say to myself, 'You know, I think she'll be good at it.' "

● ▪ ●

Jeanine's daughter, Katie, is now thirty-four. Married to a carpenter, she had a baby this year and lives in a rural area. Jeanine, now over sixty, still remembers the difficulties of raising Katie, a child with learning problems.

"All is hindsight now. I was more concerned than my husband. He felt Katie was a bright child and it would all turn out okay. Now I know he didn't want to show me how upset he was.

"School was just devastating. 'I see you are not like your sister,' teachers would say to her. She started in public nursery school in Pennsylvania. She did wonderfully in kindergarten. She was a very verbal, happy kid, a natural leader. In first grade, she started having trouble. If I had started on phonics earlier, everything might have been different. But we moved to New York when Katie was in second grade. They put her in a slow class with very disturbed children. Maybe she was babied too much—maybe we were pushing her too much. Maybe it was too much pressure because we were readers and writers. She had an overbalanced IQ. She performed well on oral skills, but on anything written she had great difficulty. We discovered the teacher would make her stand in a wastebasket. She never told me till years later.

"The next year they decided she should go into a bright class. In the bright class she learned to chat. They just didn't know what to do with Katie. She could not spell—she'd put letters in but they were all jumbled. The other kids were really nasty. She'd get so angry she'd throw her book and scream, 'I hate books.' Meanwhile, she gained weight and was terribly unhappy.

"I was so upset. I would cry all night. I worried about her. We talked about it all the time. What will she do? We tried to work with her. You'd see her tighten up. She would have a temper tantrum.

"Her happiest times were the summers. We had a house and later she went to an overnight art camp. She seemed talented artistically.

"Once we tried a reading clinic. It did not help much. Then we sent her to a special school. After one semester, she said, 'It's not for me,' so we yanked her out. In sixth grade, the teacher wanted to keep her back. I felt awful. When they got their report cards at the end of the year, all the kids asked, 'Who is your teacher next year?' She said, 'They liked me so much, they are keeping me back.' My heart went out to her.

"No matter how open the family, these kids learn to hide the failures and pretend they don't matter. After a while, she didn't want to do anything. She got through junior high, but she couldn't read or spell. They slid her through.

"The school recommended psychiatric help when Katie was about nine or ten. We took her to a nice woman once a week. Katie didn't feel she helped. She was very kind, but Katie went because she thought it would please us.

"Of all my children, I'm closest to her. Katie's like my best friend. She's extremely loyal. She would give you the shirt off her back, even if she didn't have one. She's more that way than the other kids.

"I felt maybe I had the same problem. I still have trouble spelling. I read fast, but even today, I will mispronounce. A child spends so much time in school, no matter how good the parenting, it takes a terrible toll. There is pain for a mother in seeing a child perform poorly in school.

"You always feel for your children. People judge you by your children. But the child has to find what they want in order to be happy. My immediate friends always thought she was bright. Even now, my friends always say, 'First, how's Katie? What a great person she is. She's so very warm.'

"I do think our marriage was stressed. The first year she wasn't learning to read—I was sure I was to blame. It made me feel terrible. She'd put up a brick wall; she wouldn't talk. You didn't know she was hurting until she suddenly burst into tears.

"Now she has lots of friends—a whole life. She feels success through her baby. My husband and I have been married for forty years. We helped each other through this. But it was always emotional for us as parents.

"People who meet Katie today would be surprised to know she had all these problems. But we hurt for her. I sensed that she was unhappy, but there was no way to change it. I'm just grateful she is happy today, but I wish we could have saved her all that pain."

• ▪ •

Although hearing the experience of others can provide support by showing us the universality of our dilemmas, most mothers want more. They want to know what they can do to make matters better.

There are, indeed, things to do. Studies show that the presence of a learning disability does not doom a child. Interestingly, there is a subgroup of children with learning disabilities that does even better than their non-learning-disabled classmates. What brings success, it seems, is that these youngsters feel good about themselves.

The children who do well take responsibility for themselves. They internalize the locus of control. Children who are not as successful blame themselves for their failures but never take credit for their successes.

Building self-esteem is not easy; the task is lifelong. Because frustrations and difficulties are inevitable, a mother must first learn to identify and manage her own conflicting feelings.

2

Coping with a Mother's Feelings: The Psychological Side

I did not have trouble accepting that my children had a problem, but I wanted a problem I could see, confront, and conquer. This problem was so vague and disparate. It was hard to set realistic expectations. It was hard to know what was a learning disability and what was poor teaching; what was just daydreaming and what was attention-deficit disorder; what was hyperactivity and what was a lack of discipline; what they will naturally outgrow and what needs professional attention.

Because my children are both good-looking and charming, I always had lingering doubts: Am I making a mountain out of a molehill? Have I just been too impatient, too demanding? Am I stigmatizing them? Are the "experts" really right?

Other mothers told me of similar doubts. One divorced mother of a nine-year-old boy explained:

> My older sister has a son who was not diagnosed until the fourth grade. He was always high-strung, given to temper tantrums. He actually seemed to have more problems than my son. But my sister never put him in a special school. My own son was terrific by comparison, so my sister and my mom wondered why I was putting him in a special setting. "Are you sure you're not making it a bigger deal than it is?" they'd ask. They felt I wasn't handling it right. So, I'd get off the phone with them and begin to reevaluate it all over again. It was very confusing and never really clear.

"We go through hell and no one knows it," remarked a widow whose fourteen-year-old dyslexic son was just conquering his reading problem when I mentioned I was writing this book. The truth is most special mothers do experience an emotional upheaval. They have feelings they are not always proud of, indeed, feelings they may be ashamed of and loathe to admit to anyone.

Because mothers are usually the ones who spend the greatest time raising and relating to the child, these feelings are sometimes not even understood by their spouses. In talking to scores of mothers for this book, I was struck by the intensity of the mothers' feelings. I remember one marvelous mother of a fourteen-year-old boy. She taught children with learning difficulties for many years. I knew mothers of her students who, without fail, raved about her calm and organized approach, her unique talent with these children. She seemed to me the model mother for such a child. Yet, when speaking of her own son, she showed the same intensity and frustration that I had seen so often and surely knew myself.

Raising a child with learning difficulties can be a lonely experience. I spoke with older mothers who linked their loneliness to the fact that until recently little was known about learning disabilities. However, even today's young mothers expressed this same lonely feeling.

Our children also have intense feelings. The child feels a mixture of anger, frustration, guilt, and depression. He feels angry at the demands made of him, demands he cannot meet. At the same time, he blames himself for not being able to do what he wants to do. He feels humiliated and angry at others—parents, teachers, and friends—who see him always struggling. To complicate matters, as mothers, we absorb and reflect our child's feelings.

Almost all mothers, at some time, experience the following emotions:

- Disappointment
- Fatigue
- Guilt
- Anger

- Depression
- Confusion
- Frustration

Like all mothers, I dreamed of a child who not only combined all of our good qualities, but was even better: better looking, a better athlete, more musical, more artistic. For nine months, I had loved our idealized child. With the discovery of learning problems, this dream was shattered. It felt like a death. It was powerful and painful. Most mothers of children with learning disabilities go through a similar process. One mother explained her feeling this way:

> For me, I think there was a feeling of profound disappointment. This was a second marriage for my husband. He had two older children who had had a divorce imposed upon them. They had been very affected by it. Our son was a very loved child in a very strong union. We thought he would be very different from them, that things would be totally right this time. He was imbued with all of those fantasies. And the fantasy was very strong. Then he was such a marvelous, delightful baby . . . so bright, so independent, so competent. It was such a shock when he developed serious reading problems. When I realized he was just a mere mortal and he'd probably have as hard a time as the older boys, just in another way, it was very, very painful.

At some point, we all must lose our idealized selves, confront and accept our real selves—warts and all. We must take the same journey in relation to our spouses . . . and our children. The farther our dreams are from reality, the more arduous is the emotional mountain we must climb.

Condemnation is the last thing mothers need. Yet, it is too often the first barrier met by mothers. The "with-a-mother-like-that-what-do-you-expect" attitude is pervasive. I remember one particular incident when my son was in kindergarten. I had volunteered to accompany the children on a class trip. On the way back to school, we stopped at the park so the children could play. All the children scrambled up the jungle gym. All but mine. My son would climb one rung, almost fall off, and go back down. Whereas the other children scrambled up without seeming effort, it was hard for him. I could see it.

"Why doesn't my son climb the way the other children do?" I asked his kindergarten teacher, a woman I liked and respected. The teacher looked at me and said, "You don't love him enough." I remember the tears that involuntarily welled up in my eyes.

The hurt and pain of seeing our children struggle is intensified when we are blamed and condemned as the cause. It is a double assault. When we need help and support, we often receive just the opposite.

Not only do others blame us but, most painful of all, we blame ourselves. Nothing seems to go hand in hand with motherhood as closely as guilt. Most mothers feel guilty that they are not as supportive and nurturing as they'd like to be. Children with learning problems need greater patience, so mothers may feel even more guilt. Although I hate to admit it, sometimes I would say mean, hurtful things to my children and then feel just awful. "Now that was a stupid thing to do," I'd yell in frustration, or "Why don't you think for a change?" This is not to excuse such behavior, but simply to explain that mothers are only human after all. Because I worried that the children might be behind, I felt a constant pressure to help them catch up. I should be doing more was the ever-present feeling.

Some women feel guilt for somehow causing the problem. One described her lingering doubt this way:

> When I was three months pregnant, my husband and I went for a vacation in Arizona. One day, I sat for a long time in a Jacuzzi, talking to a friend. I have always wondered whether that hot water, during that crucial time in my pregnancy, did something to the brain cells. My husband says impossible, my pediatrician says no, but it sticks in my mind. Is all this really my fault?

Since a mother-child relationship is lifelong, it is not surprising that many mothers feel deep concern when they discover their children not only have problems but seem to have problems that may affect many aspects of their lives. One woman whose only child, a son now fourteen, has learning disabilities put it this way:

> For me, depression was not a stage but something that continually came and went, based mainly on my child's progress and also what I perceived as the status of other children his age.
>
> A learning-disabilities specialist advised me, when he was still in kindergarten, "Enjoy and love Damian for what he is. Don't compare him with other children or you will always be unhappy." I have remembered this advice for years, but doing it is difficult. Because I know that seeing him in contrast with other children is emotionally stressful, I find myself dreading school plays or camp shows. Of course, I go; I smile. But it is difficult for me.
>
> I remember when my son was in a first-grade show. The children had to do an "oochy-coochy" dance. They put their right foot in, their left foot out, and then spun themselves about. I could see he was struggling terribly; he was completely out of step. He watched the child next to him, but he still could not get in step. No sooner did this dance end than another formation began. Again, he tried desperately but could not do it. As a parent, my heart ached for him. The other children seemed to do it with such little effort and they got it right. He seemed to be working ten times as hard, yet was simply unable to execute the steps.

Being a special mother is just plain tiring. One mother, who began taking her son for speech therapy at age two, confessed she felt so burned-out she did not want to spend time with him once they finally returned home. Although the speech therapist had said to spend just ten minutes a day working on his speech, she found even that too much of a burden.

> I am ashamed to say it, but it is true. I tried to play with him, but because I never got any feedback that I could relate to, I gave up. But now I feel guilty. I feel if I had spent more time, his speech delay would have been less severe.

While she is struggling, a special mother cannot help but notice how easy other mothers seem to have it. They do not seem to encounter any of these conflicts. Envy pops up. While difficulties are undeniable, we must not forget the joy. Over and over, mothers told me these children were kinder, more caring, and more spiritual than children who have not struggled.

Even when my children made mistakes, there was something joyous and charming about it all. I remember one time when my son was very young and we were out hiking, I leaned over a railing. "Be careful, Mom" he shouted worriedly. "If you fall, I'll have to call 199!" Unfortunately, while the thought was exactly right, our local emergency number is 911! Another time, when his garbled speech led me to discuss speech therapy with my husband, he listened with great concern and then exclaimed with deep seriousness, "I don't see why I need peach therapy!"

Although specific feelings can be identified, most mothers experience a mixture of feelings. It reminds me of the teeter-totter I used to ride with the children in the playground. One minute I would be up in the air, happy, satisfied, and enjoying the view. Suddenly I'd hit down fast, hard, and hurting, but then I was up again. . . .

A PSYCHOLOGIST SPEAKS OUT

Making a psychological adjustment for a mother means understanding her whole mixture of feelings. Only by examining these feelings can you better handle your emotions. First and foremost, it is important to realize that a certain amount of depression, anger, and anxiety is normal and healthy. That is one of the purposes of this book. Equally important, mothers should know that the painful feelings do eventually ease as we see ways to help our kids and see them change and progress. Mothers then come out of their darkest feelings into a warmer light. But the difficulties are not outgrown like last year's winter jacket. Unfortunately, some persist.

Dr. Bob Broad, a senior clinical psychologist at the Communications Disorder Center of Mount Sinai Hospital in New York City, explains that the mother's role as ego builder is crucial for the learning-disabled child. Conveying hope, he emphasizes, is the single most important thing for these mothers, as well as for their children. While the problems resulting from learning disabilities are real, the key factor enabling a child to compensate for his real weaknesses is a strong sense of self. A child must feel confident enough to meet the task. If the mother is overwhelmed and devastated by the difficulties, the child will absorb her fear. No child can learn when he is frightened. It is the mother's task to "keep the faith" and convey confidence about the child's ability to progress and overcome.

Instilling the "you-can-do-it" attitude is not simply a matter of saying it, however. In order to have the child believe it, the mother must first truly believe it. This can be a complex task, because, as mothers, we also see real stumbling blocks. To convey confidence from our hearts and not just our mouths, we must understand some aspects of our own personalities that may be interfering with our own self-confidence.

Mothers vary widely, but Dr. Broad explains that it is good to be aware of unproductive patterns.

The narcissistic perfectionist mother may see the child's problems as a personal injury. Her conditional love is filled with all sorts of expectations. It is difficult for a mother with high perfectionist standards to be in sync with an immature and evolving child, especially one with difficulties.

Some mothers are guilt-ridden. This sort of mother may feel that she is somehow to blame for things having gone wrong. Through insight into the real nature of learning problems, her guilt can be lessened. She learns that the child's problems are unrelated to anything she has done. Not everything about a child relates to the mother's input.

Some women may feel inherently defective. When this type of woman has a child with difficulties, she may subconsciously feel it is proof of her own inadequacies. This causes low self-esteem and my lead to depression. These mothers need their children to perform successfully in order to feel good. Because this is not always possible with a learning-disabled child, these mothers may not be able to provide the emotional support these children need and deserve. In such cases, therapy for the mother may be beneficial.

Another group of mothers has difficulty with denial. The mother who continues to deny her child's problems can cause difficulties for both herself and her child. One obviously hopes for a child who is a joy, a credit to the parent. When dreams are thwarted, a mother may still hold on to this idealized vision. When the child makes an error, however, the mistake reminds the mother of the difficulty, and she flashes her rage. This may show she has not fully accepted the child she has.

Patience is an aspect that bears introspection, since it is so crucial for a mother to be patient with a learning-disabled child. Dr. Broad points out that patience is a complex dimension of personality that deals with our tolerance to frustration. A mother should be patient enough to be in tune with her child, and ahead, but not too far ahead, in her expectations.

Some mothers may unconsciously thwart their child's efforts to become more autonomous. We all, in some way, hate to see our children grow up. In a misguided wish to protect, or in an effort to prevent competitive comparisons, this kind of mother may keep her child dependent. The child may feel this conflict in the mother and not progress as he might. Again, such conflicts can be dealt with in therapy.

Finally, some mothers may think they see problems where none exists. Psychologists refer to this as the "excessively concerned parent." A mother may feel her child has learning problems because he functions below *her* expectations. The child, however, may be functioning within his own potential.

Sometimes a mother must cope with being called neurotic and overconcerned if she really feels a problem exists. A friend of mine has always felt her oldest son had a subtle memory and learning problem. On testing, the experts repeatedly said no. My friend recently told me she wants to take her son for another evaluation. I am certain the experts have called her neurotic. I know her son, and my instinct says she's probably right.

For a mother, awareness is step one. Therapy can be helpful in some cases, not only for the child but also for the mother. Our children are very sensitive to our wordless messages. As important, mothers should live as contentedly as possible. Our ease and happiness will have immense positive value for our children as well as ourselves.

3

What Is a Learning Disability Anyway?

"How did you know your child has a learning disability?" one mother asked me. "I wouldn't even know what to look for. Maybe my child has it and I don't know it."

"Oh, my kid does that too. All kids do," a friend commented. Mothers of children with learning difficulties have a sense, however, that something more than the usual is happening. "I knew very early—before he was three—but I didn't know what to call it," one mother said.

Although the label may be new, the difficulty is not. Years ago, people believed learning difficulties were caused by underlying emotional problems that consumed the child so much that he could not focus on learning. In the 1950s, the accepted theory was that learning disabilities were due to disturbed family relations. The idea was that parents had concocted the problem subconsciously to hold their marriage together. Once the marriage improved, they believed the child would be fine. In the 1960s, these children were simply considered lazy and less able. Today, experts believe learning disabilities have a physiological base; they are nobody's fault, not the parents' or the child's.

Public Law 94-142 defines a learning disability this way:

> Specific learning disability means a disorder in one or more of the basic psychological processes involved in understanding or in using language, spoken or written, which may manifest itself in an imperfect ability to listen, think, speak, read, write, spell,

or to do mathematical calculations. The term does not include children who have learning problems that are primarily the result of visual, hearing, or motor handicaps, mental retardation, emotional disturbance, or environmental, cultural, or economic disadvantage.

The Orton Dyslexia Society tells us that learning disabilities are not a disease to "have" and "be cured of," but a kind of mind. Most broadly defined, a learning-disabled child is one whose level of academic achievement is lower than would be expected on the basis of his or her intellectual potential.

Learning disability is an umbrella term describing an extremely wide variety of children. These children have average, high average, even gifted intelligence and look like all children, but they have a hidden handicap. They may have trouble receiving information through listening (auditory processing) or reading (dyslexia) or may struggle to express themselves verbally or in writing. In addition, many have difficulties in spelling, math (dyscalculia), word-retrieval (dysnomia), and concentration (attention deficit).

What does all this mean? Why would I think it applied to my child? The truth is I did not even know about learning disabilities before I had children, and never connected them to my child at all. All I knew at the beginning was that my son did not seem to be responding like other toddlers I saw. As the mother of a girl now in college recalled, "From the very beginning, I realized that somehow she wasn't exactly like every other two-year-old that she played with in the park. Slow language development was the mark that set her apart from the others. Many times we would return from a little friend's birthday party—Jessica with a fist full of balloons and chocolate ice cream all over her face, and me with carefully hidden anguish and an evening of tears once she was asleep. Nothing like a roomful of peers to bring home the point that your child can't do what every other child seems to be doing."

I also noticed small, nonspecific things that, to me, produced a disquieting picture. When I would tell my toddler to get something, he would sort of stare at me. I remember clapping my hands behind his head to see if he was deaf.

In prenursery, it was difficult getting him to join the children's games. When they played musical chairs, he did not want to join in. Even when he did, he looked close to tears. The other children would bounce happily on the trampoline, but it scared him.

I remember dreading those one-hour classes. All the other mothers seemed to be enjoying their children, and their children seemed to be having fun. My son was miserable, and I was dismayed and disturbed by it. His performance was not like theirs: they were involved, but he preferred to wander aimlessly; they were eager, but he seemed resistant; when they sat and drew, he made one line and walked away.

I was unsure, however, about the cause or the cure. Should I just let him stay home? Should I keep trying, although I had been trying for weeks without any change? Was it significant? He was only two. It seemed so silly to be upset about these small things. How could you tell someone you were worried because your two-year-old wasn't scribbling properly?

I wondered if I was unduly concerned. My husband would tell me, "I never even went to kindergarten and I did alright. It's ridiculous." Secretly, I felt that my personality and my mothering were at fault. What else could explain it?

One weekend my parents were visiting from out of town. My mother volunteered to take Mark to his class. At first I hesitated, thinking of all my difficulties. But then I thought it was a great idea. I hoped that Grandma would do the magic. If it worked, I decided I would hire a babysitter and limit my input as much as possible.

I truly expected things to be better. Grandma was calm and had been a teacher. Unfortunately, when they returned, I knew things had not gone well. She seemed hesitant to say anything at first. I could see she was upset.

"I just could not get Mark to do anything," she said. "I don't know why. He just would not join in. I feel terrible and I'm exhausted. I just don't understand it." I knew her feelings: the exhaustion, puzzlement, and self-blame. We sat down and talked. We were both puzzled.

So the following year, when the nursery school suggested testing, I felt, in a strange way, relieved. Given all the crosscurrents, I looked forward to, at last, "the answer." I took Mark for testing in May. The test was supposed to take one hour. After four one-hour sessions that spread from May through September, we finally met with the chief child psychologist, who was a very famous woman, but who had never even met my son. We were not allowed to speak with the psychologist who actually did the testing. We were told she did not consult with parents. So here we were, four months later, sitting in front of a marvelous fireplace, speaking with this lovely, perfectly charming woman who had never even seen our son.

She was judging him from test scores but, to me, my son was not the sum of his scores. To me, who loved with a mother's intensity; it was that special "him" I cared so deeply about. That she could speak about him when she had never even seen him not only bothered me, it hurt me.

She told us that Mark did not play properly and that all his difficulties resulted from this. She could not tell us exactly why this occurred or what it meant. He had been difficult to test, she explained. She never mentioned the term learning disability or discussed a special school. What she did say was that Mark should repeat kindergarten.

At the time, it made sense to me. Since Mark would be switching to a new school, it would be easy to begin in kindergarten rather than the first grade at the new school. When we left, his problem seemed like a rather small thing. I had the feeling he was a little behind but would surely catch up. When we reapplied for kindergarten, however, the schools immediately wanted to know what was the matter. They gave Mark additional testing. It was at that further testing that they pointed out all sorts of things he did not do but should. They were the ones who explained learning disabilities to us and strongly recommended a special school. It was difficult for us to put Mark in a special school before he had attended a regular school, but we felt it was better to get help too early rather than too late. I now think it was the best thing we did for him.

DANGER SIGNS

What is a typical kid? What is just immaturity? What might reflect a learning handicap? Because all children are unique, these questions are extremely difficult to evaluate. Pamela Reiss, director of the Learning Disabilities Clinic at Mount Sinai Hospital in New York City, explains: "Parents often have an innate sense that there may be a problem. However, sometimes they wait. My advice is not to wait. We can always rule out problems, but for a difficulty it is better to find out early and get services early."

Exactly what will a mother see? Many mothers I interviewed said they just knew something was wrong. It is just something a mother feels. When I asked mothers to tell me what they noticed, they mentioned the following signs. (*Please note:* These traits were noted by various mothers: *every child did not show every trait.* One trait does not suggest a learning disability. However, a number of symptoms may suggest a need for further information about the child.)

- *He could not learn the alphabet.* It took *years* for him to memorize the whole thing. First he could not even remember *A.* I'd put the letters up in his room, on the refrigerator, but he still could not remember.
- *He could not write his name, tie his shoe, button his shirt, cut, or color.*
- *He didn't understand childhood jokes.* You know those childhood standards . . . "How do you make time fly?" Well, he'd just look blank. He never laughed because he never understood.
- *He'd ask the same questions over and over.* Everyday he'd ask, "When is tomorrow? Is this tomorrow?" It drove me crazy.
- *His answers were off base, unconnected.*
- *He had a great deal of trouble learning to tell time.*
- *He was hard to understand.* I was always asking, "What?" I could not just listen; it took real patience and effort. His explanations were jumbled, hard to follow.
- *He was a difficult baby.* He'd whine incessantly, cry easily. He was frightened, timid, supersensitive.
- *Things seemed to float over him.* When he was very young, I noticed he was not learning everyday things. My husband said,

"You just have to teach him more." But I could see things were just not being absorbed.

- *He made funny word mix-ups.* I thought these were funny, but he got angry when I laughed.
- *He could not tell right from left.* A successful family court judge, who is dyslexic, recalled, "I never knew which hand to put over my heart when we recited the Pledge of Allegiance."
- *He lacked affection. He rarely smiled.*
- *He was socially out of it.* He was not invited to anything. It killed me to see him so hurt. But it started very early.
- *It was hard for him to play board games.* He'd get confused in counting and moving the pieces. At first, I thought he was cheating because he'd skip or land in between. Then I realized he didn't know where to land.
- *He had trouble remembering words.* They were common words—words he definitely knew.
- *He reversed all his numbers and letters.* In first grade, he wrote a composition with all his numbers and letters reversed—even the letters in his name. I already suspected a problem, but this made me take action.

Not only does the mother notice something, the child himself notices. Children are harsh self-labelers. They see that other children know the answer, while they may feel unsure and confused. One eight-year-old girl eloquently explained that she was "down low," while all the other children were in higher groups "on higher ground." She said she felt like she "was red and everyone else in the whole world was green." Another child described feeling like a "tight little ball, all closed up inside." Surely this is painful—psychologists say some of these children suffer from a chronic low-level depression.

A child's reaction is not based only on the nature and severity of his problem. It is affected greatly by his personality, the degree of the difficulty, and his parents' reaction to the difficulty. The child's intelligence, his other strengths, and the quality of remedial services also affect his reaction. Sometimes children repress their feelings until they become adolescents; then their anger, resentment, and depression may surface with powerful force.

What causes a learning disability? Experts still are not certain. They do know that heredity is a factor in a large percentage of cases. It may be passed down genetically; often a father, grandfather, uncle, cousin, or other relative had similar difficulties.

External factors before, during, or after birth may be the cause. During pregnancy, toxemia, poor placental attachment, alcoholism, taking certain drugs, or infection may be responsible. A long and difficult delivery, a breech delivery, umbilical cord around the neck, dry birth, intracranial pressure due to forceps delivery, or poor position in the uterus are birth traumas that can cause learning disabilities. After birth, high fever, meningitis, a sharp blow to the head, lead poisoning, or oxygen deprivation from respiratory distress all can produce these difficulties.

Although parents are told not to dwell on the cause, most mothers I spoke with did think about it. After all, that is a natural reaction. Unfortunately, several mothers carried a lingering self-blame, which was probably both inaccurate and harmful. One woman even mentioned wondering if her child's learning problems were the result of something sexual she and her husband had done during pregnancy. (No studies show a sexual act as a cause.) In my interviewing—not a scientific sampling—I noticed fathers generally expressed less self-blame.

If a mother feels overwhelmed by her child, if she notices things that concern her, or if a teacher alerts her to a difficulty, it is essential she seek help. A child does not simply outgrow these difficulties. The first and best thing for a mother to do is to consult a pediatrician.

A PEDIATRICIAN'S DIAGNOSIS

A pediatrician can evaluate whether a child is performing below developmental norms. This may be confusing for a mother because a child with learning disabilities does make progress. Therefore, a mother might resist the notion that her child has special needs. But these children do not keep up with the very specific developmental markers established by the American Academy of Pediatrics.

Any child who is having problems learning should have a complete medical examination. Physical problems can interfere with learning. For example, allergies may cause inattention; anemia can produce lethargy; hypoglycemia, glandular problems, or seizures may give the appearance of daydreaming. Eye and hearing examinations are essential. Approximately 3 percent of school-age children have a hearing impairment. Because the familiar Snellen Eye Chart assesses only central vision acuity, a more detailed eye examination is needed. The tendency to reverse letters is not usually caused by a vision problem, however.

A speech difficulty may be the first sign of a learning problem. If your pediatrician answers your concern about your child's speech at age two or three with remarks like "Don't worry, Einstein was a later talker too" or "Why should he talk? You anticipate his every wish", you should get a second opinion. These are out-of-date remarks. The "normal child, anxious mother" diagnosis is also inappropriate. Mothers' concerns should be taken seriously. Some physicians can inhibit the flow of information if they appear rushed or impatient. If the doctor does not appear interested in pursuing the problem, the mother should not "forget it." Current research suggests that the application of intervention techniques at a very early age can maximize a child's potential. Often mothers are the first to notice the problem and the primary one to seek help. So if the mother "drops the ball," it seems almost inevitable that both she and her child will suffer. Studies show that the longer the disorder goes untreated, the less positive the outcome.

Doctors, however, cannot be totally blamed if a child's problems are misdiagnosed. Unfortunately, the signs of a learning disability can be easily confused with other problems. Even experts do not agree exactly what test can accurately diagnose learning disabilities.

Susan Levitzky, M.D., a respected pediatrician in New York City, explains that informing the mother must be done gently, with a respect for her difficulties and anxieties. Because the problem is hidden, mothers often blame themselves for causing it either by not spending enough time with the child or by using the wrong child-rearing techniques—being too strict or too permissive. In her practice, she has noticed that the working mother will immediately say she should quit her job. Learning disabilities are not a mother's fault. They are no one's fault. Quitting work will not solve the problem, although scheduling adjustments must be made to accommodate the needed tutoring and various therapies.

Dr. Levitzky stresses she is always positive and reassuring; she feels a pediatrician is very important in helping the mother advocate for the child and in giving the mother the needed emotional strength to fulfill the child's many needs. She likes to call it a learning "problem" because the word "problem" also means there are "solutions."

She recommends seeking an activity that will allow the child to achieve outside of school. For example, most of these children enjoy noncompetitive sports. Art, pottery, sculpture, and carpentry are satisfying, individualistic outlets, and she recommends community service as another activity with great positive feedback. Besides helping others, it puts the child in touch with children in youth-service organizations who share similar values.

I asked Dr. Levitzky if there is one thing, more than any other, she would advise mothers. Without hesitation, she said, "The main role of the mother is to have the child get through with a feeling of self-worth. Low self-esteem is the biggest deterrent to success in life."

Today, drugs are sometimes prescribed for children with learning disabilities, but a learning disability, in and of itself, does not indicate a need for medication. Most psychiatrists and pediatricians believe that drug therapy should be used only in conjunction with other kinds of supportive services. They feel many children with subtle to moderate learning problems can be trained to concentrate and overcome their problems without the use of drugs. Of course, a child must have a complete evaluation to know what is best in each individual case. Drugs do not make a child smarter; they just make him more able to concentrate. According to studies, children taking these drugs show no improvement on school achievement tests.

Some drugs, specifically stimulant drugs like Ritalin and Dexedrine, are very effective for hyperactive children. All hyperactive children are not wild and unmanageable, as the label conjures up. To a pediatrician, the syndrome—*hyper* means excessive—may indicate constant, purposeless, unproductive motion: the child who is endlessly drumming on the table or tapping a pencil. One mother, whose child did such tapping, decided to give him drum lessons. It worked wonderfully, and he has shown a real talent for the instrument!

Mothers I know who have given their children these drugs are staunch advocates. They feel it made their child able, for the first time, to listen, concentrate, and learn. The reason for the widespread (some say too widespread) use of these drugs is their effectiveness. A 1976 study suggested that 35 to 50 percent of hyperactive children showed dramatic improvement, 30 to 40 percent showed moderate benefit, and 15 to 20 percent showed no benefit. Some studies have shown up to an 80 percent success rate.

Many mothers feel uncomfortable giving their children any drug. One mother, who refused drug recommendations, told me, "I didn't want to give him the message that popping a pill was the way to solve his tension; I also felt if he took it, he might have a sense that he didn't do it, the drugs did. I thought it would interfere with his sense of mastery. And, I worried about long-range effects."

Side effects—insomnia, poor appetite, dry mouth—must be taken into account. Although these are usually short term and tend to occur only at the beginning of treatment, these drugs must be monitored at least every few months. They cannot just be given and forgotten; medication-free periods are essential. Some parents discontinue drug therapy during the summer, resume in September, and then stop altogether when the child reaches adolescence. Some hyperactive symptoms spontaneously disappear at adolescence.

Unfortunately, some studies indicate these drugs may affect growth. One study showed growth inhibition in children who were taking Ritalin for more than three years. This should be taken into account for the poor eater or small child. (*Note:* not all learning-disabled children are hyperactive and not all hyperactive children have learning disabilities. An evaluation by a pediatrician, when considering any drug therapy, is essential.)

IS SPECIAL EDUCATION THE ANSWER?

Good teachers are important for all children; they are vital for these children. For a child, a good teacher not only brings the excitement of learning but also builds the confidence that is an essential first step. Insensitive teachers can be tremendously destructive. One mother recalled a first-grade teacher who, day after day, would hold up her son's papers to the entire class as an example of poor work. The teacher explained she did this because she felt he was bright but "lazy" and this would discipline him and make him work harder. Of course, it never worked and these incidents are still remembered as painful by this boy, now a man in his thirties.

Even the best regular teaching techniques might not succeed with dyslexic children, however. They need a multidisciplinary, multisensory teaching approach.

One mother said she could not imagine how a child with special needs could thrive without special education. She admitted she just thought her son was "thick" before his special education. Of course, she still loved him, but she worried constantly about his future—his emotional and educational well-being. Special education changed not only him but also her perception of him.

> It reminded me of having a body that is a box. There were things in the box, but they could not come out. Wouldn't it be terrible to spend your life as a closed box? With special education, they were able to open the lid and pull out all the beauty in him. Once I knew he had it . . . that there was so much there, I was not as anxious or worried because I knew that the box was open and he could work with what he has. And, he has more than I ever even hoped.

To treat these children differently is not to discriminate against them, but rather to make certain they have an equal chance.

Special education can be a double-edged sword, however. A learning specialist told of a visit to a special class in a large inner-city junior high school. When she walked in, all the children shouted, "Shut the door, shut the door!" She could not imagine what was wrong. Later, the teacher explained the children were embarrassed to have any passing friends see them in the special class. Certainly being labeled and removed from the mainstream has emotional ramifications. There can be just plain physical problems too. One mother told how her child's school did not have a special class. Because her daughter had so many needs, she was going back and forth, ten to fifteen times a day, to the resource room and other specialists. She was so segmented in her programming, she was becoming utterly confused. An outgoing child, she was always stopping in the hall to chat and getting to every specialist late. Over and over, she heard her name announced over the PA system (what she called "the noise box") because the teacher became worried when she did not arrive. She felt singled out as "the person who was always late."

Ideally, special education stresses the organizational strategies and basic skills students with learning difficulties need. Unfortunately, these special classes are sometimes poorly disciplined and just catchalls for children with a variety of problems. Expectations may be reduced too much, affecting motivation.

A Brighton, New York, school district has just instituted an interesting innovative program in which the resource room teacher works along with the regular teacher in the regular English/Social Studies class. She helps the children right in the classroom, so there is no disruption with student travel, the work is coordinated, and the child does not sacrifice the stimulation of his peers. It seems to be very successful.

Gail Cartenuto, a teacher of children with learning disabilities and physical impairments, offers some very special insights on special education. Ms. Cartenuto, a cerebral palsy victim, went through school in special education classes until high school. She now teaches a class of twelve children (five out of the twelve are physically handicapped, as well as learning disabled), ages four to seven. She explains that by state law there can be no more than a three-year age range in any class.

Ms. Cartenuto feels that if a child is being considered for special education in the public school system but the need for special services is still in question, the mother should advocate for a regular class placement first. In the early years, she explains, this provides more stimulation, giving the child greater benefit even if he is not absorbing all the material.

Once a child has had special education and is ready for mainstreaming, Ms. Cartenuto recommends doing it gradually, perhaps with one class a term, beginning with a nonacademic class so the child can acclimate to the new setting and demands. She reminisces how she herself was in an orthopedic special class and then suddenly mainstreamed into a large city high school. After being in a sheltered environment, she found this sudden change very difficult, particularly the social adjustment. Since the parent must be consulted when a child is mainstreamed, he or she might request gradual mainstreaming.

If our children cover such a wide spectrum from the gifted to the low-average in intelligence, and each family is so unique and complex, how can relevant advice really be given? Wisely, Dr. Levitzky points out that "While the children may vary, the goal for all of them and their mothers is the same: helping each child to develop to his or her fullest potential."

4

What Should I Tell My Child? How Can I Help?

Years ago, learning disabilities were treated as a deep secret. Today, they are out of the closet. Nevertheless, I was not happy attaching a label to my son. What should I tell him? It is a dilemma all mothers face.

Because he began special school in the first grade and all his friends went to different schools, I wondered if I needed to say anything at all. I felt my words might hurt him deeply. I worried if I didn't explain it properly, he might misunderstand. And even if I did say something, what should it be? I could not just point to reading and say, "You are having a tough time—here's why." Because he was so young, the professionals kept using the phrase "at risk." I didn't want my words or theirs to become a self-fulfilling prophecy.

Uncertain how to handle this delicate dilemma, I asked the director of my son's special school. She felt I definitely had to say something and told me, "When he asks, it will be the right time and you will know what to say."

I remember it well: I was getting ready for my very first book interview on nationwide TV. As I was nervously dressing, my son came in and said, "Steve told me our school is a special school and all the kids at the school are there because they have problems. What's my problem?" Although the director had promised me the right time, I could not imagine this was what she meant. In any case, I simply and honestly explained that some people who tested him thought he may develop problems in reading and math, so we decided to put him in a school where they were expert at teaching these subjects. He listened carefully. His response almost brought tears to my eyes. He told me he did not care what kind of school it was; he really liked the kids and the teachers. He was happy there and that was all that mattered.

Experts stress it is important to be open and honest. You should not take a child off to a room for a formal talk, but treat the problem in an everyday manner. A good time to start a discussion is when the child is confronting a difficulty. As a child gets older, beyond age nine or ten, he needs to understand his strengths and weaknesses, so he can advocate for himself.

For all children, the message should be, "How can we help you with this?"

Sometimes, mothers worry that telling a child will be such a blow he will lose all self-confidence. When things become difficult, he may give up, believing he will never succeed anyway. Mothers fear it may confirm the child's deepest worry—something really is wrong with me. Although these thoughts go through a mother's mind, psychiatrists say, for most children, understanding their difficulties provides relief. It lets the child know he is not "stupid" and that help is available. It gives the child a chance to explore his fears and misconceptions, and place himself on a solid psychological foundation.

Actress Susan Hampshire was diagnosed as learning-disabled at age thirty. When asked whether she felt that knowing early on that her difficulties had a name would have made things easier, she said, "absolutely." In her book, *Susan's Story,* she wrote

> It would have been easier just knowing that I was not mentally retarded, or lazy, or backward, or emotionally disturbed, but that the small part of my brain, governing language, was not functioning well. To know that it was not a disease, but a disability, a condition that could be improved, would have made all the difference.

Most mothers I spoke with for this book used a tell-but-don't-dwell approach. They explained areas of weakness to their children but emphasized approaches and strategies that help.

One mother, herself dyslexic and the mother of three children with learning disabilities, tells her children, "We all have difficulties and this is yours. We all have allergies too. You sneeze and you get on with life." As she explained, "They're able to look at their learning problems the same way."

The danger of labeling must be addressed. In hindsight, I feel I was very naive. I willingly placed my children in a special school thinking it would provide the soundest educational foundation. When it came to mainstreaming, however, I found a great deal of stereotyping, even among educators. They would generalize about "these kids" in a way that was both prejudicial and inaccurate.

Although the whole field of learning disabilities is openly discussed, there is still prejudice. I remember going to a small dinner party when my son was in second grade. The conversation, as it often does, got around to private schools. One man expressed great dismay that his daughter's school was now taking children with learning disabilities. When I asked what was the matter with that, he shot back, "How would you like your son sitting next to some retard?" Surely, if this man had known of our son's problem, he would never have said this, but prejudice exists, whether spoken or unspoken.

Labels can hurt our children's chances for college admission and job placement. One learning specialist told me of a bright, mildly dyslexic student who applied to eight competitive colleges. On four applications he mentioned his learning disability; on the other four he did not. He was rejected by all four schools where he identified his problem, and accepted by the other four equally competitive schools. This doesn't mean we should try to sneak our children in and slip them through with as little notice as possible (what one mother dubbed "the slide and glide" approach), but we must protect them from prejudice.

These children need supportive services, but, they should receive this help, if at all possible, without labels. If the child must get Board of Education services, a parent must make certain the school has the required Individual Education Plan, which describes the services to be offered, and provides for an annual review. When the child has completed the treatment, he should be removed from the classification of handicapped, and parents must be notified of this action. It is important for a parent to check permanent school records to make sure there is no continuing designation unless services continue.

Sometimes people who meet my son for the first time are amazed to learn he has learning difficulties. Many wonder if they were simply developmental problems he had but outgrew naturally. In retrospect, I feel some aspects of my son's difficulties were developmental; however, the early special education services he received were crucial to his gratifying development. I know if we had waited, this progress just would not have happened. It was the result of hard work, his hard work, and I respect him for it.

Another theory I hear is that these children are just dumb: the learning disability label is simply a euphemism, an excuse. I am sympathetic to this view because I think it would have been my opinion if I had no personal experience with learning disabilities. To me, it was fascinating to see that these children who come from different backgrounds do tend to make similar mistakes and have similar problems. When some of these children came to our house, I was always amazed by their similarities.

When our younger son's class took a boat ride on the Hudson River, the captain let each child take a turn at steering. All the children had a terrible time telling right from left. But rather than teasing one another, they were all laughing and enjoying their confusion. They were able to admit their difficulty and then work on it. If our children can accept their own problems in this spirit, it will be an invaluable lesson.

When a mother is told her child has a learning difficulty, her first instinct is to help—to teach her child. Yet, teachers at my son's nursery school strongly urged me not to do this. "You be the mother, let the teachers teach," they said. When I protested that I seemed to work easily with my son, they countered that I was causing deep, irreparable emotional damage even if I did not realize it. They also said if I taught him, I'd be making him dependent forever. Their opinions were firm and strong.

Following their recommendation, but against my gut feeling, my husband and I hired an educational therapist who came to our home once a week. During the lessons, I'd hear my son throwing things (something I was stricter about); at the end of the session, she'd have him draw a picture. No matter what he drew, she would say, "I can see you enjoyed working on that" or "I can see you worked hard on that." This was just not my style. I expected more. I would ask him what he wanted to draw and, if it was a house, I would make suggestions (Does it have windows? Is there a door?) until it was somewhat finished. When I complained, however, I was told her approach was correct: I had too high expectations.

The high cost of these sessions also bothered me. I could not understand what they were accomplishing. Finally, I told my husband I was going to stop these visits and teach him myself. I didn't care what the professionals said.

I began by making a list of *at* words—*bat, hat, fat, cat.* He seemed to catch on. I could see that teaching him was not that hard: the only thing was, he had to be shown everything. But I learned much the same way, so I could relate to it.

Interestingly, I taught him phonics, which the experts now strongly recommend for dyslexics. One reading specialist told me that if you teach a dyslexic by a sight-word approach, he will never learn to read. Of course, I did not know any of that at the time. All I knew was that, more than anything, I wanted my son to succeed, and I was going to show him everything that worked for me.

A friend told me to get the Dr. Seuss books. I bought *The Cat in the Hat.* It was the first book he read, and it was not easy for him. But he did it, and we both felt terrific. After that, I continued working with him. Through the years, I would sit with him and show him how to study and how to outline.

I never did the work for him nor did this become an issue. He wanted to work; he just needed help. My son seemed to find directions difficult. Once he understood what was required, and the knack of going about it, he would work hard and eventually produce good results.

Although I worked with him, I always had inner conflicts about it. Indeed, I wondered if I was causing deep psychological damage. It was not a farfetched idea because I did not always work with patience (and that's putting it kindly!). The fact is when I became frustrated, I did the entire litany of sins: I yelled, I sighed, I got silent, I looked totally exasperated.

But somehow, despite it all, we were a team. He kept asking for help and I kept working with him. In the morning, after he left for school, I promised myself I'd be more gentle, more patient, but it did not always happen. It was frustrating for me. He was smart. I could see it. When he understood something it was almost as if a light went on in his eyes. One minute he'd understand a complex concept and say something that was clever and insightful, better than anything I could think of, and the next minute he would misunderstand something totally simple and obvious. For example, one day he was given the following assignment: "Read 'The Necklace' by Guy de Maupassant." He asked me what that meant. I did not see how he could possibly be confused. Then he showed me that it was the third story in his book, and he wanted to know if he was supposed to read the first two stories as well. All of a sudden, I saw his problem in a different light. It was sequencing; the fact that the teacher had assigned the third story confused him. I often ran into this kind of illogic—actually, it was logic, once you saw it from his point of view, but it was just not the usual perspective. In a way, I found these mistakes fascinating; the teachers, however, were much less loving about it. They would give him an "incomplete" if he did the wrong thing. Once, he stayed up very late doing pages one through six. The teacher said briskly, "I didn't ask for that; you were supposed to do problems one and six."

Sometimes all my efforts resulted in almost comical scenarios. I remember when my son was in the seventh grade and about to have a social studies test on the explorers. Because memorizing random facts was difficult for him, I tried to get him to use memory tricks and mnemonic devices—a strategy that had worked for me. Before I realized it, *I* was working very hard and had just about succeeded in memorizing all the explorers. But when I looked up, he was not doing anything; in fact, he was looking out the window. At the time, I phoned a friend to stop myself from throwing the book at him, but I also saw the humor in the situation!

It was only in doing research for this book that I realized that theories on parental participation had changed. Joan Knight, an esteemed New York City reading specialist who teaches dyslexic children age nine and older as well as adults, believes parents owe it to their children to help them. She conducts citywide workshops for parents on techniques for teaching their children to read. The mother of a dyslexic daughter, she advocates working daily (even ten minutes will make a difference) with a child.

Indeed, I would have thought that I had discovered the solution if I did not have two children. Despite my newfound confidence, I could not teach my younger son, Greg, at all. First, he was very resistant. I urged him to read street signs but he refused. I tried the *at* words and the Dr. Seuss books, but nothing worked. When I asked him to read a word that started with the letter *t*, he would guess wildly, giving neither a *t* word nor even something that fit in with the story. I could not tell where his ideas were coming from. A second-grade teacher whom he adored taught him to read. I will always be deeply grateful because I know no matter how hard I would have tried, I just never could have done it!

When I saw the wonderful breakthrough progress with his decoding, I was ecstatic. Greg still had trouble with comprehension, and his teacher had to stop often to focus on the meaning, but his progress gave me confidence that things were improving. More important, it gave him confidence. You could see it in his whole being.

Not only are all children different, but with my sons, I found that what worked wonderfully at one stage did not continue to succeed. As Mark approached adolescence, he paradoxically seemed to want my help but he was resistant as soon as I started to give it. "Oh, forget it, never mind" was what I would hear, and he'd walk away, leaving me feeling unsettled.

Even in the best of times, parent tutoring is definitely not for everyone. One friend of mine felt that she failed whenever she tried to be something other than a mother—tutor, psychiatrist, or friend—to her children. Her advice, after being a special mother for twenty years, was "Be there, listen, and support. That's a mother's role, but nothing else."

In all this mother talk, we must not forget fathers. One woman explained that throughout elementary school, both she and her husband tutored their son; each took three subjects. She said it gave all of them a very supportive feeling. Should a mother teach her child? I think a mother has a very good instinct about what works best, for herself and her child. While it is helpful to be aware of pervasive professional wisdom, I think she should follow that instinct.

DEALING WITH THE SCHOOL—DELICATELY, OF COURSE

Perhaps nothing is more important to a child's progress than what he does every day in school, but dealing with the school is not always easy. "It's a delicate balancing act," one mother of a public school student told me. "It's hard, working with the teachers. You don't want your child to fail, but you also don't want him known as 'that kid with that horrible mother.' " The mother of a private school student remarked, "The minute you say 'something,' the school sees your child as a problem. If the school would motivate and interest the children, they would learn. But immediately, the school views any type of learning difficulty negatively. It becomes a problem . . . a problem child and a problem mother."

Another mother felt her requests for help produced more negatives than positives. When she saw her son struggling with homework, she called his teacher, so he could be helped with organization and study skills. Although the teacher spoke with him, there was no follow-through. The mother said the problem landed right back in her lap: all she felt she had accomplished was making her son look bad. She decided not to be as forthcoming in the future.

In my own experience, I found it was very difficult working with the school, even the special school. Some experts urge mothers to fight and pressure. In theory I agree, but in practice, it is not so easy. You have to be careful about causing resentments. The tactic that worked best for me was placement changes. The few times I was able to change teachers or groups, it made a significant difference.

One extraordinary mother whose son is now a college graduate told me that the special education department of her public school had asked her to speak to a parents' group years after her own son had graduated. At the meeting, she was dismayed to find that parents were "griping about the same things we fought to have improved fifteen years earlier." Although she had spent a great amount of energy dealing with the school and had obtained good, successful programs, she discovered they had all been dropped. "That's what frustrates me most," she remarked. "Things just don't change."

SHOULD I KEEP MY CHILD BACK?

Most children in our country are educated in a relatively smooth progression through the grades in their neighborhood school. Few parental decisions or interventions are needed. For the mother of a child with learning disabilities, however, much greater involvement is required. Educators sometimes suggest repeating a grade to buy time for these children, who mature later than their peers and may not be ready for the work of the next grade.

Some experts strongly suggest repeating kindergarten. A landmark study by the Gesell Institute of Human Development at Yale University showed that "unready" students never really catch up. They warned against the common response "He's a bit immature now, but he's bound to catch up." Because experts found that starting school a year later can make an immense difference for children who are not ready, they extolled the advantages of early retention, or, as they called it, "the gift of time."

In the 1980s, the percentage of children who were retained in kindergarten, rather than promoted to first grade, jumped significantly. In some states, almost 10 percent of all public school children were repeating kindergarten.

Dr. Louise Bates Ames, associate director of the Gesell Institute, has said, "We maintain that even if it is traumatic to keep them back, it's better to traumatize them once and get it over with, than have them face problems every day for the next twelve years."

However, today, the educational pendulum seems to be shifting away from repeating in the very early elementary years. We now realize that the emotional stress on both parent and child of having to repeat kindergarten is not as short-lived as educators once believed. These children are often teased. What's worse, they view themselves as "not as good" as those who advance. Numerous studies show that teachers respond to them negatively, too. Teachers are affected by test scores and labels. One teacher reportedly gave his students more challenging assignments after he saw a roster with numbers from 130 to 150 after their names. He thought these numbers represented their IQs, only to find out later that these were their locker numbers!

Certainly, just repeating something that did not work the first time will not necessarily solve the problem. A parent must know why the child is not mastering the material.

Betty Osman, an esteemed learning specialist in Westchester County, New York, and the author of *Learning Disabilities: A Family Affair,* states, "To justify retaining a youngster in a grade higher than kindergarten or first grade, one should be able to predict that the child would be consistently performing at least in the middle or, better yet, near the top of the class by next year. If it seems he will still be on the bottom in academic skills, I'd seriously question the advisability of such a move."

My personal experience with retention has left me with mixed feelings. Our son Mark repeated a year when he was mainstreamed after sixth grade. This was done with almost all the children who came from special schools. Academically, it was a success. Mark was placed in the higher academic group, and he performed in the upper-quarter of this group. Because he had been in an ungraded school, the curriculum was not repetitious.

Socially, however, it was problematic. While there may be little difference between a junior and senior in high school, there is a significant physical and maturational gap between a sixth- and seventh-grader. During the first six months, he continually complained and asked to be put in his proper grade. It did not seem an appropriate social placement to me either, but the school wanted to be certain of his academic skills. Mark did attain a leadership position in his class and was even elected class president.

However, there was always a lingering doubt in my mind whether this retention was really for the best. And there were unexpected ramifications. The first thing the children asked when the camp bus pulled in was "What grade are you in?" It placed him in an awkward position—lie or explain. Neither seemed right.

Unfortunately, for some children, repeating one grade is not enough, especially if a child was retained in kindergarten or first grade, before hard-core academics began. One very bright eleven-year-old had a severe reading difficulty, so he repeated first grade. However, when his reading did not improve as hoped, he transferred to a special school. Despite intensive tutoring and special education, decoding was still painfully difficult for him. When it came time for him to be mainstreamed, the regular schools felt his reading skills were just not adequate for their academic demands. They wanted him to repeat again. "I won't do it, and you can't make me," the child cried in hurt and defiance.

While a parent might accept retention, most children absolutely hate the idea. A talented and successful adult dyslexic told me she felt dumb from the moment she was told she had to repeat third grade. Surely the emotional repercussions of retention cannot be underestimated.

WHAT SHOULD I TELL THE CAMP DIRECTOR?

Dealing with learning difficulties involves more than school. Should a mother tell a camp director about a child's problems? Many mothers feel the camp might not accept the child, preferring to avoid any possible problems. I felt very unsure what to do because my children were both well liked and their difficulties were academic. I did not want to present them in an unflattering light.

Unsure, I asked a friend whose dyslexic twelve-year-old had always been in regular school. She recommended explaining difficulties without labels. She said she always tells the camp director about her son's messiness and short temper, and at the same time shares her suggestions for the best way to handle these difficulties. She felt that problems without positive suggestions were not that helpful.

For some mothers, medication presents an awkward situation.

One mother confessed she worried about it all the way to camp. But when she arrived, the camp nurse told her very matter-of-factly to add her son's name, medication, and dosage to the list. When she explained the medication schedule to his counselor, she found some unexpected positive benefits. Rather than being negative, the counselor took a special interest, almost as if now he had a mission to help this child.

Most experts advise communicating with the camp director. If he or she is not sensitive, mothers would certainly want to be aware of this when evaluating the camp. Even a caring director must be informed in order to prevent misunderstandings.

● ■ ●

Sometimes I felt tired of dealing with it all. So I was relieved to read Priscilla Vail's column in a recent Orton Dyslexia Society newsletter, in which she wrote of the fine line between caring and letting be. She stated, "Once the support systems are in place, it is important for parents to avoid panic at each small evidence of overflow. Giving over the problem to the student and the teacher implies trust, and well-founded trust is a precious gift."

One mother of four learning-disabled children was asked by the chairman of her local committee on the handicapped how she maintained her calmness. She simply explained, "Long ago, I decided if it was something I knew they'd master by age twenty-one, I decided to forget about it."

I certainly know how frustrating it is when problems already battled rear their heads again. As one mother said, "It can begin to dominate your life." But I strongly feel that sometimes it is better to do nothing. This is not, as I dreaded at one time, a matter of losing ground. There are times when mothers need just plain time-out; Our children need it too!

I remember taking my children to their favorite hill on a beautiful, snowy, winter afternoon. Clinging to my brave son in front, we went flying down the hill on an inner tube. Believe me, I didn't think a thing about learning disabilities. It was survival I was worried about!

5

A Marriage Under Stress

Dealing with learning disabilities had wider ripples than my relationship with my children: It had a powerful impact on my marriage. When I married, I found my marriage affirmed my view of myself in a very positive way.

When my children developed problems, however, my negative feelings about myself rushed to the forefront. Suddenly, I felt emotionally thrust back to second and third grade. The feelings of being out of control, of not knowing the answer, came rushing forward.

I did not like being placed in this situation. "I feel like I'm in nursery school again, and I hated nursery school," I would tell my husband. He seemed unsympathetic. "You are not in nursery school and to feel that way is ridiculous. It is their problem, not yours." But I found the separation difficult to make. Each time they would tell me about a hurtful event, or I saw them struggling in school, I felt their pain. I often thought I felt it twice, for I was seeing my own pain as well as theirs. My marriage had somehow become inexorably intertwined with this struggle.

In the early years, my husband and I had found our interests and intellectual levels remarkably similar. We each had careers that we found enjoyable and challenging.

Just as our children's problems affected my feelings about myself, they also changed the tone of our marriage. All of a sudden, my needs were different; I needed my husband's emotional support. But he was a pragmatist; he wanted to give quick answers to problems that did not seem to have ready answers. He did not like discussing issues without solutions. "Are you bringing that up again?" he would ask with annoyance. "I thought we finished that last night." This attitude would somehow exaggerate my needs. Suddenly, our always pleasurable relationship felt strained.

My conversation became totally fixated on the children. I became obsessed with them. I could not go to the movies or to dinner without eventually bringing up the subject. It was impossible for me to just make a decision concerning schooling or tutoring, and then forget it. At the end of a demanding day, more problems were the last thing he wanted when he walked in the door.

We had opposite views about professional advice. Because he is a professional, his instinct was to believe what they said. However, what they said did not always fit with what I observed in my sons. I felt almost crazed. I was determined to do what I felt was best, regardless of the professional advice. When we left an evaluator's office, we would argue. "You are always putting the children down," he would say to me. But I did not see special education as a negative; rather, I viewed it as something that would save them by ending their confusion. My husband was happy if the evaluator said, "He'll catch on, it's just taking him a bit more time." But the thought of leaving things alone panicked me, since I could see an increasing confusion. I kept thinking, if we wait, there would be no catching up.

One woman related her experiences during a similar turbulent period. Teachers were always winking at her and saying, "Bright boy; he's having trouble now, but he'll be fine." Her husband was shouting "Stop looking at him every minute," and her own instinct was saying "He's just not getting it." She was desperately trying to cover first math, then reading, then spelling, but was not able to get everywhere fast enough. She described the marital stress: "We had always been so close, so solid. He was an involved father. Suddenly, I found we talked but we didn't really talk. I walked on eggshells because I wanted everything to be wonderful and beautiful. I wanted things to be nice." Things first improved when their son went to a special prep school where the teaching was on target and his needs were met at last.

Likewise, in our marriage, there was a marked improvement

when both children were finally in special school. Things greatly improved as the children matured and we saw wonderful progress. While we disagreed when things were bad, we both recognized the improvement. We could see, at last, that we were on the right road.

A fifty-year-old advertising executive recalled her son's early years this way:

> It was very difficult for my husband. From the time our son, John, was very, very young, we had trouble with him. He was small, a crier: he would not eat. He'd fall a lot; he had more stitches than any kid on the block. He'd climb up things. He was fearless, but he couldn't see the consequences of his actions.
>
> He got thrown out of day camp, sent home from birthday parties. We took him to a psychologist. He's the one who said he's hyperactive. It affected me. I felt terrible, but my husband took it personally. He took it as if something was the matter with him.
>
> We'd hide from each other. He felt nothing was wrong. I wanted to get help—but he never believed in psychiatry. But, eventually, I did send John to a psychiatrist. My husband would rant and rave about them not knowing a thing. Then he'd carry on about the bills. "They can wait," he'd shout, but the doctors would complain to me.
>
> When they told us John had to repeat kindergarten, it was awful. My husband would internalize it: I'd talk to the world. But whenever he heard me talking about John, he'd get angry. But I couldn't talk to him; he just did not want to hear it. He would never talk about John. There was so much silent disagreement between us—clenching-of-the-teeth silence. I wouldn't say anything because I knew he was under a lot of pressure at work. I discovered it was better not to talk to him. But I always felt like I was so alone. After a while, it was coloring our whole marriage.

While all parents know they should act united, the reality is sometimes far from this ideal. Different coping styles can become exaggerated, leading to divisiveness. As one mother explained:

> My husband and I differ a lot. He feels she should do what she wants, and I feel she needs firm guidelines. I am constantly trying to redirect her. But my husband just lets it happen, lets it all skate by. So, I become the bad one, and he is the good one.

"I'd definitely go with my father, if you got divorced," my daughter tells me. Sure it hurts.

A child's problems can intensify marital frictions. One woman said whenever she and her husband had a dinnertime argument, their son would become agitated and upset. Before they knew it, they'd start to yell at him and, too frequently, he became the scapegoat.

> I am good at giving directions, sometimes too good. But my husband is very laid-back. I'd complain he wasn't directing the children enough. The more persistent I became, the more he'd look down at his plate. My son would feel the heat and begin to react. Soon, I was into "How can you let him do that?" I am sure, subconsciously, I did not want to confront our own problems, but really, it only made matters worse. Our problems just got pushed deeper, and our son became more and more "the bad one." The thing that helped us was therapy. It showed me the way I was manipulating things.

Some mothers run into difficulties because their husbands refuse to acknowledge their child's problems. Psychologists say that denial occurs because a parent may overidentify with a child and subconsciously fear that the child's problems reflect that they are also less than perfect. Rather than face the guilt and emotional turmoil this engenders, a parent may simply deny the problem. But if a father denies difficulties, it may leave the mother feeling unsupported and uncertain.

Parents who do recognize difficulties may, in their confusion, turn to blaming. " 'The kids sure didn't get this from me,' " one woman remembers her husband yelling in a memorable incident in the family car. " 'It had to come from you. Look at the way you are disorganized. With a mother like you, what do you expect?' The words hit like a sharp knife, just at a time when I needed a warm hug."

For a woman, there may also be a sexual response. One mother, whose hyperactive son did not sleep nights and had thrown their household into turmoil, felt she just could not handle another child. She became terrified of another pregnancy. Yet, this is definitely not the response of all women. One woman commented, "It did not really change our sexual feeling for each other or our sex life. If anything, it made it better."

A mother of four conceived her fourth child after her son's learning disabilities became very apparent. I was curious that she did not have any reluctance. "No," she explained, "we very much wanted another child. Part of it was I already knew Rick was less capable. It didn't feel right to make him the baby too. Also, my husband and I didn't like the number three; four gave us a sense of being even. And I feel that we had become fixated on Rick. We needed to step back and change our focus."

I spoke with many divorced women. Not one blamed her child for the divorce. Yet, the children blamed themselves. One ten-year-old dyslexic boy echoed the thoughts of many, saying, "When Mom and Dad first got divorced, I thought it was all my fault. I felt that for a long time. I felt like I should have been quieter; I shouldn't have been so bad. I shouldn't have been rude at the table. I felt that I couldn't tell my mom. I got so upset, I couldn't stand it anymore, so I finally told her. Then she bought all these books and read them to me, and then I understood."

One mother, now divorced, felt strongly that although her child's disabilities did not cause the divorce they undoubtedly added stress to her marriage.

Jessica was in first grade. Her teacher picked her difficulty up. She told me, "Your child has a problem. She is just memorizing the words on the page." I had her tested and they told me she had learning disabilities and would definitely need a special school. It was an emergency and a major problem for the whole family. It's a terribly difficult thing for a mother to be told. It was emotionally devastating for me, but the most pressing problem was finding a school. In those days, the choice was very limited and I wanted the best place for her. There was absolutely nothing near us. The trip would have been way too much for her. So, we decided we had to move to be nearer the school. We moved an hour away from our old house; it meant thirty minutes for her to school.

It was a major trauma and a very disruptive time for the entire family. We had a house that my husband just loved. It was on a golf course. He worked very, very hard. He was from a poor family and this was, after all those difficult years, at last, the home of his dreams. Moving was traumatic. Our new house was not nearly as nice. My husband had a longer commute. The cost of the school placed a financial strain on him. My older son had to change schools. He was still young—third grade—but it was tough on him. Does it stress a marriage? It sure does!

Anne Bobrick, a certified psychiatric social worker who taught family therapy at both the Ackerman Institute and The Payne Whitney Clinic in New York City, feels it is very helpful for mothers to be aware of common harmful family patterns so these can be avoided and to understand ways the family can manage the inevitable stresses. She describes how, at the beginning, rather than talking out fears, many husbands and wives start to fight. She describes a common pattern where a mother trying to help her son who is struggling in school suggests extra work, but the child objects. The husband, hearing the child's complaints, says she is pressuring him too much. Although they are both concerned, both trying to help, they end up fighting and hurting each other.

Rather than fight, which splits a family, Ms. Bobrick suggests that the couple should try to express their tender feelings—their fears and vulnerabilities—so they can join together and try to find ways, together, to help solve the problem.

She makes mothers aware of another common pattern: when the inevitable fighting begins, couples may sometimes find it easier and more comfortable to blame the child for the difficulties. To make a child feel he is the cause of his parents' unhappiness, however, is not only inaccurate, it is a destructive psychological blow. Ms. Bobrick reminds mothers that the difficulties are not the child's fault but the result of the couple's inability to be intimate and cope, in a united way, with difficulties.

It is important for mothers to understand what are universal feelings, as Ms. Bobrick explains:

> All parents have dreams for their children. When a parent sees a problem with her child, it causes stress. Parents get scared, sad, and often a combination of both. In their anxiety, their

thoughts often rush to the future and they wonder how their
child will ever be able to make a living.

In a family, one person cannot be hurting without it affecting
everyone. A child's problem cannot be isolated, to the child or
even the mother. A child with a learning problem is definitely
a family problem.

The media and TV sitcoms often convey a picture of the ease of
mothering, but this is not realistic. Raising any child is a difficult
and demanding task.

All children need a great deal of emotional nourishment. A child
with learning problems may need even more. Emotional nourishment is like the foundation of a house. It is crucial to all that
follows. Children without any learning difficulties may seem to
have no problems at all; however, sometimes the child may secretly
suffer feelings of loneliness and depression. In many ways, mothers of children with learning difficulties are lucky. Our children
demand attention.

Therapy is often recommended for special families. Many mothers I interviewed said working with a therapist made a tremendous
difference in the child, the family, indeed, the whole atmosphere
at home. One of the biggest advantages of therapy is it reminds
parents, preoccupied by their child, to be alert to their own individual needs, as well as their needs as an adult couple. It unites
parents.

Although therapy can and should be a positive experience, the
wrong therapist can create just the opposite. One mother recalled
how it almost pulled her strong marriage apart, saying, "When our
son was having such trouble in school, they referred him to this
psychiatrist, chairman of the department at an esteemed medical
center. Our son went each week, but we had to go once a month.
At our first meeting, I will never forget his telling me, 'Rose, you're
an overinvolved mother.' I deeply resented it, but felt I better not
show it since he was the esteemed professional.

"We had always had a good marriage, but when the psychiatrist
said this, my husband seemed to agree. It was as if they were both
pointing the finger at me. After we left his office, we had the

biggest fight of our marriage. I jumped out of the car as we were getting off the expressway. I felt out of control: what does it mean to be an overinvolved mother? I was enraged, but I was also filled with guilt. After a while, I didn't know how to act in my own house. If he was struggling with homework, I'd sit outside his door, worrying but afraid to help him. Each time we had our meeting with the psychiatrist, we fought terribly. Only when we stopped going were we able to begin mending things between us."

Several mothers, on the other hand, found their child's difficulty pulled the family back together, strengthening the marriage and making the family closer than ever. When I spoke with the fathers, they echoed these feelings. The men said it gave the marriage a united goal; they no longer bickered about little things; everything was focused on helping their child overcome this stumbling block.

When parents join forces, the family can be a very powerful unit. Of the women who were able to deal with this problem positively, all told me they faced the crisis as a united couple. As one mother put it, "In our case, we were equally frustrated, equally surprised, but we could commiserate. I felt able to tell my husband everything that happened—the good and the very annoying. If you can complain without having your spouse judging you, these things are not as big a problem as they might at first seem. We'd laugh about it and scream about it . . . but we did it together!"

6

Siblings: A Mothering Minefield

I'd like to say that when Greg's problems were discovered, I was confident and knew just what to do because I had already been through it once. The truth is I was more devastated than I had been before with Mark. Part of the reason was that I absolutely never expected it.

Greg was a bright-eyed, responsive, adorable baby. He looked like a little fighter with sparkle. He would say very clever things. I remember when he came home from his first day of nursery school I asked, "Did you raise your hand in school, like you should?"

"Why should I raise my hand?" my city-raised, three-year-old responded, "I don't need a taxi in school."

The difficulty I expected was that he might read better and faster than his older brother, presenting an awkward family situation.

The first time Greg was anything but adorable was about the time he entered nursery school and began saying "what-cha-ma-call-it" many times a day when referring to common objects; I remember joking about having the only three-year-old with Alzheimer's! Although I laughed about it, I asked his teacher, since he said what-cha-ma-call-it so often. She had noticed it, but felt it was unimportant.

That summer Mark had to do some reading-readiness, so I decided to practice letters with Greg. First, I gave him just two letters: *A* and *B*. I told him, "This is *A,* this is *B.*" He obviously understood, but after a minute he could not remember their names. I had never experienced anything like it. Thinking immediately of what-cha-ma-call-it, I wondered if it was possible he didn't have a memory.

Realizing memory is so important in early learning, I panicked. Immediately, I phoned our nursery school director. She told me not to do anything. I still remember her exact words: "I won't touch it with a ten-foot pole." She said not to teach him anything; we'd look at it again in the fall, when he would be four years old. When school resumed, I mentioned my concerns to his teacher. She listened, met with me after two weeks, and said she felt it was common for mothers who had one child with a learning difficulty to "see it" in the next. She saw nothing and told me to "relax."

Still worried, however, I decided on a tactic. There was a public school for the gifted in our area, where many students in Greg's class were applying. It required a standardized test, which was given at a center near us. I decided to apply and have my son tested, just as so many mothers of children in his class were doing. I decided to say nothing about Mark because I did not want to color the results. I would apply like everyone else—just another upwardly mobile mother with a child who, of course, was—what else—gifted.

I took him for testing. He cried during the test. At the parents' evaluation conference, they mentioned the crying, but said perhaps he was tired. They gave us a kind of graph, which reminded me of my childhood drawings of the Swiss Alps: a series of high peaks and low valleys. The evaluator explained that looking at these results, he would immediately think of learning disabilities. In our son's case, however, he was certain it was simply immaturity.

As we walked home, my husband said, "You see, there's nothing to worry about. He said it's not a learning disability, it's just immaturity." But my immediate reaction was "I knew it, he's got learning disabilities."

I was quite certain not so much of the label but that he had a poor memory or some sort of problem that seemed to be getting in the way. I could feel it when I tried to teach him.

Despite my firm conviction, I also had great ambivalence. Am I crazy? Am I making him crazy? The teachers and evaluators must know: they see so many children. Maybe I'm somehow perceiving things wrong. On a subconscious level, I am certain I did not want it to be; I just did not have the emotional energy to do it all again. Indeed, I often felt the only thing I learned from my previous experience was "Boy, I never want to go through this again."

So, after nursery school, Greg went to a regular first grade. I did mention my concerns to the school. They saw, of course, a charming, cute (he hates that word, but he was) child. The teacher noticed all the reversals, but she told me reversals were not unusual at his age. She also noticed that he was very serious (as she put it, like someone taking the law boards), but she said this was because I was overanxious.

It was an expensive, small private school in New York City: the first thing they taught the first-graders to do was to write a check! After they got that important matter out of the way and the year progressed, I saw Greg's learning becoming confused. He had trouble with number concepts, but the curriculum moved rapidly from addition to subtraction. Soon he was totally befuddled by both. He did not want to try to read and, when he did, he just guessed randomly at words, regardless of sound or meaning. When teachers asked him to write down his thoughts, his compositions were difficult to follow, yet the teacher would only write "Can you explain?" and draw a smiley face.

Although I was concerned with the academics, I was much more dismayed about what I called Greg's "being." He seemed sad, downcast. His personality, always spunky and devilish, was somehow losing its sparkle. I remember feeling that he was growing "down" rather than "up"; the joy was disappearing. As a mother, seeing this caused me pain—pain that perhaps was emotional, but it felt almost physical. It was hard for me to see him like that. I felt compelled to get him to a better place.

I wish I could say I was calm, thoughtful, and reasoned in seeking a solution but the truth is I was angry, resentful, frustrated, and panicked. Yet I was determined to change things.

I consulted a child psychiatrist who told me Greg should stay in regular school but that I needed therapy. I probably did, but I was becoming more convinced that the solution was special education.

It was doing marvelous things for Mark. That year he had the most wonderful teacher, and because I greatly respected her I asked her about Greg. She did not know him, but I outlined all my concerns and all the professional advice. If in doubt she said she would definitely get good, early special education. She felt it could only help.

After speaking with her, I took Greg to Mark's school for an evaluation. Reviewing the results, the educational director concluded his need for special education was "unequivocal." His year in regular school had not only left him on the preprimer level in all areas but had also defeated him in subtle ways because it had confused him. "Why did you wait so long?" she asked. It was hard to explain or understand myself.

Although I had been through the experience before, I somehow felt all the same conflicts again. I had always considered myself a smart person, one who learns from experience. But it was an emotional journey for me as a mother, personal and intense each time.

When I notified the school that Greg would be transferring, the reading specialist sent us a letter saying she felt we were doing our son "irreparable harm" by placing him in special education. Of course, by then, we had made our decision. But I could not just dismiss her words. I was not that sure of myself. When, at first, his class at special school was not to my liking, her words plagued me.

After a while, however, I saw that the special school did for Greg what it had done for Mark; it brought back the joy. He ran down the street again. It worked. I could definitely see it. It ended my ambivalence and conflict. All the problems were not magically solved, of course, but he was, once again, happy, willing to try, and excited about doing things. To me, that's what counted.

I remember attending a parents' meeting when Mark first entered the school. One couple had two children there. I remember thinking to myself, "Those poor parents!" I never imagined it would happen to me, but I also never imagined the positives, and there were some significant ones.

A wonderful closeness developed between the boys. Things that might have been awkward, such as tutoring and retention, became just the norm. They played at about the same intellectual and athletic levels, so they enjoyed being together.

Although I felt my sons' shared sensitivities brought them together, another mother of two learning-disabled boys had just the opposite experience. "I think because both had frustrations, it heightened and exaggerated their way of dealing with and viewing each other," she explained. When her older son was fifteen and in the ninth grade, she sent him to one of the outstanding special boarding schools and felt it had both academic and family benefits. "I think he enjoyed the autonomy of being away and it focused him. If everyone was studying from seven-thirty to nine-thirty, he did too. At home, he spent too much time and energy checking what his brother was doing . . . who got more TV time, who had more homework."

She found that separating her sons did not end their rivalry, however. Her older son, who had always been the family tennis player, became jealous when his brother took up the sport. "Tennis is my sport; he's tall, he should play basketball," he'd shout. Although his mother laughed when telling the story to me, she said the issue still comes up; the anger and jealousy are still there.

A significant number of children with learning disabilities are adopted. Learning disabilities may be caused by maternal malnutrition, poor maternal care, complications at birth, or hereditary factors. Regardless of the cause, it complicates sibling relations. "I wish I was the one you borned," one woman remembers her daughter saying. When the natural child becomes the achiever, it places an even greater wedge between siblings. The dynamic of one child falling into the role of the "good" child, the "achieving" child, and the child with learning difficulties becoming the "problem" child is troublesome. As mothers we know this, but learning difficulties may mold such a pattern anyway.

Vulnerabilities can be used by two very different siblings in hurtful ways. "My son was always an achiever. He was fascinated by politics," a mother of two explained. "Because of my daughter's learning disabilities, she does not enjoy discussing world issues. She values it but, at the same time, she tries to devalue it and put

it down. She's more social, more aggressive, but when she's unhappy, she'll lash out where he's vulnerable. He gets deeply hurt.
I can understand it, but it is painful to watch."

In many families, the "good" child also pays a psychological
price. The sibling without difficulties may have what is dubbed a
pseudodisability, becoming the hidden victim of the problem.
There is often resentment at all the additional attention and time
given to the child with learning difficulties.

The "good" child may be forced into a demanding role. One
mother told me how her daughter, who excelled academically and
was a student leader, often acted as a buffer in the family. She
helped her brother with his homework and was much more patient
than either parent. She also explained her brother's behavior to
their parents in a very supportive way. While she seemed to do this
in good spirit, psychiatrists say siblings, like parents, must be allowed to identify and understand all their complex and conflicting
feelings—the understanding as well as the irritation.

One mother of four, whose son with learning problems was
popular among his classmates, said she found no sibling implications. "John always went to his tutor. He rode his bike over, only
occasionally complained about it, but in every other way he was
just like the other kids. In fact, he was the easiest to get along with.
They all thought so."

Intense love-hate sibling relationships may develop. As children
mature, their constellation of difficulties becomes interwoven in
their actions and reactions. One mother gave an account of the
complexities arising from her son's low self-esteem and poor ability to relate cause and effect. Recently, she went on a business trip
with her husband, leaving explicit instructions that her sons—a
boy with learning disabilities, now eighteen, and his brother just
ten months younger—could each have a friend over, but no par-
ties.

However, her older son, always eager for the role of "Mr. Popular," spread the word (without telling his brother) that the apartment would be "open." Hordes of teenagers, most of whom he did
not know, came, drank beer, crowded the place, and even danger-
ously threw some things off the balcony. Once they started arriv-

ing, the younger brother realized what had happened, but was unable to stop things.

Upon their return, the parents were placed in a serious dilemma. Their older boy was supposed to leave the next day to be an outward-bound camp counselor. The mother knew it would be best if he went—best not only for him but also best for his younger brother. She decided to deal with the incident seriously at the end of camp. After camp, however, he was on his way to his freshman year in a special college program.

This mother explained that at her son's therapeutic nursery they had taught the children to excuse away their defeats with "it-was-just-not-my-day" type of thinking. It saved the child's self-esteem. Yet, as her son matured, he continued this thinking. It became an escape from responsibility. Interestingly, studies by psychiatrists of learning-disabled adults show they may continue to blame their troubles on factors beyond their control and deny personal responsibility.

Despite being a direct mother with solid values, this woman sent her son off to college with no strong punishment aside from the usual lecture. "All his life," she said, "crises always happened at just the wrong time."

The pain of the mother whose only child has learning disabilities can be particularly poignant. It may be difficult for her to gauge the problem because she has no one else with whom to compare the child.

One inspiring mother, whose only child, a daughter now twelve, is severely learning-disabled and reads at the first-grade level, told me, "I never went through the 'why me' stage. I have had good acceptance. I tell parents, 'Don't dwell on the negatives.' Sure we see them and there is not much we can do about them. Let's concentrate on the positives. I tell the school, 'My child has these needs. Now, what are we going to do about it?' If she is not getting the programs she needs, that's when I get upset. That's when I'll fight like a she-cat."

I certainly cannot deny that it was hard for me to have both my children struggling in school. It was particularly stressful on the day of parent-teacher conferences. I just could never get myself in the right emotional spot. When they were young, I always found the reports disappointing. It reminded me of those people at the state fair who sit on high stools and, if the beanbag hits just right, are suddenly dunked into a bin of cold water. Even though they are expecting it, it is still a cold shock.

As my sons matured and the results of special services took hold, however, the reports improved. And by then, although it sounds trite, I had come to realize that all people have troubles and most are more serious than learning difficulties.

Recently, I attended an Orton Dyslexia Society lecture for parents on siblings. I sat next to a very pretty young woman, who looked just like the actress Amy Irving. I pictured her child as one of those adorable frizzy-haired kids in overalls. She was just that kind of mother. I secretly thought, "Her son is probably four and not reading yet, and she's concerned."

When we spoke after the meeting, the common question of how old are your children and where are they in school came up. She explained she had two boys, nine and eleven. Both had learning disabilities. I was intrigued. It sounded so similar to my situation. However, she went on to explain that both her boys also had muscular dystrophy. They were not wheelchair-bound but were unable to use the stairs, and both required an elevator. For her, the physical setup of the school was crucial, since both boys were in middle school and changed classes. She had them in a good public school, where they did not have to go great distances daily for lunch, gym, and locker.

She told me friends would say, "I don't know if I could cope if I were you." But she told me, "Of course I cope and they would too. There is no choice." She was very concerned with keeping her sons involved and getting them the best possible programs. "They are great kids, they deserve it," she said.

Immediately, my children's problems seemed insignificant. I felt incredibly lucky.

7

What Works:
Advice from Other Mothers

While all mothers know the difficulties, what we want is help. I was tired of detailed diagnoses. They were passive. I wanted something active. I wanted something that worked. So I asked each mother I interviewed to tell me not only her feelings but also what worked.

When I asked one mother "what works?" she instantly said "reading to him." Interestingly, when I interviewed her son weeks earlier and asked, "What do you like best that your mom does," he instantly replied, "She reads to me before bed each night. Some kids think it's babyish, but I think it's fun. It gives me good dreams." Experts agree that these children benefit from the vast reservoir of information bedtime reading provides. Jason's mother explained:

> I started when he was just a year old. He's now almost twelve, and we still do it. Even when it's late or I'm very tired, we read one page just to preserve the nightly ritual. At one point, I was concerned that I was reading too much, that, as a poor reader, he was becoming dependent on me. But I think there is more benefit than harm. He talks about the books as if he has read them. Intellectually, he learns things he could not learn on his own.
>
> It is a quiet time and we discuss many things that are not in the book. It gives us a chance to really talk. Just last week, Jason told me when he reads, he loses the train of thought—he is so busy decoding. I am always wanting to help him catch up. It is a pressure I constantly feel, so this is great for both of us.

> When I got divorced, the reading was a real bond. At the
> beginning, we were both dreadfully aware a third person was
> missing. So, at dinner, we'd even bring the book to the table.
> We'd read a bit and it really helped us in the transition. It was
> as if there were not just the two of us, but many more characters
> with us too. It created something that was bonding us and
> interesting us, besides just being a mother and child.

Another mother found that what worked best was urging her son
to use people as resources. "If he wanted to know what someone
was doing, I encouraged him to go up and ask. Today he feels
comfortable talking to people, and I think this skill, although origi-
nally a compensatory one, might be his greatest strength."

Stressing artistic abilities is yet another thing that works. For me,
it was fascinating that, at age three, my younger son, who would
write *u* for *n*, would also spaciously transfer a flat object to three
dimensions. When I told him to draw a large apartment building,
he somehow mounted a folded paper into a flat piece, creating a
fabulous paper tower instead of the ordinary tall building I had
envisioned. In *Their World*, an inspiring magazine published by the
National Center for Learning Disabilities, an architect related how
he believed dyslexia was his gift because it enabled him to see
objects in three dimensions. A mother whose child drew amazing
cartoons at age ten told me, "We always made him feel this was
a very valuable form of expression, and I gave him lots of art
materials to work with. I think it was a real source of pleasure, as
well as self-esteem."

"The thing that saved me, I think, was the special school," explained one mother, who also admitted her strong early reluctance
to use special education. I would certainly agree.

Mothers do not want their children to feel different. Because this
is a painful feeling we instinctively try to shield our children from
it. Professionals told me that when recommending remedial services, either special school or resource room, this was always the
parents' first concern. Parents would say, "I don't want my child
to feel different," or "he'll be embarrassed if his friends know he
goes to a special school," or "he'll be teased by the other kids."

Because we lived in New York City, which provides diverse educational settings, these thoughts were of less concern to me than the idea that my son might reason along these lines: These kids are dumb (children see things in such black-and-white terms). My parents put me here. Therefore, I must be dumb, too. For our family, the decision was difficult, but in hindsight I feel it was the single most important thing we did.

At the school, he met many children—terrific kids—who shared his difficulties. This quelled self-doubts better than any lectures about "feeling good about yourself." Because the teachers were skilled and the program was geared to his needs, he began an upward spiral of competence and confidence, whereas before he seemed set in a downward spiral of poor skills, lack of confidence, and great upset for him and me. Not only did the special school work for him, it also worked for me. Because he seemed happier, I was happier.

Other mothers stressed the importance of finding not just a special school, but the right special school. One mother explained that her son attended a special school, but he was still a tremendous problem. At a different special school, she found, he was much more successful.

This school knows what they are doing. He's programmed; everything is carefully monitored. He never did sports before; now he's on the soccer team. Even at the other special school, he was incorrigible, out of control. They left everything to me. He was supposed to go to a homework tutor, but he'd run away. I never knew where he was. When I got a phone call at work at three-thirty each day, I knew it was the tutor; I knew he had not shown up. From that moment on, I could not concentrate on my work. I was losing clients; I was afraid of losing my job.

But this school has changed everything. It gets him involved. He's excited about projects. He has an adviser, the soccer coach, who sees him everyday. He does his homework. Before, I must tell you, all I wanted was for him to disappear; literally, I never wanted to see him again. I wanted him away. I wanted him to go to boarding school seven days a week and never come home for vacations. I'm laughing now, but I was serious. I got to hate him. This school has given me my kid back. He's found his self-esteem. I can love him again. I want to walk into my house again. Believe me, the right school, the right environment, can make all the difference. When it's working, you know it.

Sometimes help can come from the most unexpected source. I feel that getting a dog was one of the best things we did for our younger son. Greg wanted a dog, so one afternoon we found ourselves buying a black-and-white puppy (and wondering what we were getting ourselves into). The dog was a tremendous hit from the first. The dog was always there, endlessly loving, supportive, and uncritical. Whenever kids came over, they loved to play with the dog. While we all adored the dog, it definitely favored Greg, sleeping on his bed and greeting him happily each day. It was, and still is, a wonderful plus in his life.

Not all animal stories end so happily. There was a beloved "fat kid" in the school who always did the unusual. He told me he got a monkey but had to get rid of it because the monkey tried to strangle his mother! Telling the tale made everyone, including his mother, roar with laughter. The whole class even made a special trip to the local zoo just to visit the monkey!

A small but positive change occurred when I started saying "thank-you" for even the littlest things my children did. I made an effort and sometimes overdid it. But this small sign of gratitude had a remarkable way of diffusing anger and tension. My children soon picked up the cue and started saying "thank-you" to others. It was a small thing, but it seemed to make a noticeable difference.

Homework time is difficult for all mothers. I find my older son starts his homework at just about the time I think he should be finishing it. He stays up late and I seem unable to get him into an earlier schedule. One mother told me about a method she devised that works very well for her family.

> I have set up a quiet time in our home each weekday night from seven to nine-thirty. It's just like prep school. Starting promptly at seven, the boys must each go into their rooms and do their work. They cannot make or accept phone calls, and their friends know it. They cannot watch TV. There are no exceptions. I find that children struggling with their own disorder thrive on imposed order.

One mother who just had a baby by her second husband and also has a fourteen-year-old boy with learning difficulties explained:

> The best thing I did for everyone was to set very definite limits and stick to them. I was loving, but very, very firm.
>
> For example, for a while my son's bedtime was eight-thirty but he'd try to manipulate it. He'd come in the kitchen at eight-twenty-five for his snack, but I would not budge. He'd yell; he said it was stupid, but I never backed down. I'd tell him, "I said it and I mean it." Normally, this is not my nature. My home was liberal, flexible. It sounds petty, but one specialist said it was just like a speeding or parking ticket. It is very specific; if you drive one mile an hour too fast, or park one minute too long, there are consequences. The limits must be absolutely fixed.
>
> As we tried it, I saw it worked; it made less friction in the family. Things were calmer.

Over and over, mothers mentioned that the more they talked about themselves and their children, the more information, understanding, and support they received. "You realize there is a large number of people who share this problem, once you are open enough to discuss it," one mother explained. "I definitely felt less alone and less to blame because I saw so many similarities in others' stories. Truthfully, the best part is you find yours isn't the worst case. I would come away thinking I don't have it bad at all."

Other mothers mentioned that they found joining a support group was more helpful than just "friend-talk." Although parents can commiserate, often they really don't know what to do. A professional who acts as a group leader can make specific suggestions that can then be evaluated at the next session.

One public school special education teacher told me her attempts to organize a mothers' group were unsuccessful. Mothers would say, "My child is nothing like Alice," perhaps a more impaired child. They did not want their children linked to children who had more serious difficulties. Support groups associated with local dyslexic associations might be preferred by some mothers (see the listings in Appendix B).

I once joined a special mothers' group at the local Y. Unfortunately, the children had a wide variety of difficulties: autism,

Down's syndrome, emotional instability, and hyperactivity. I empathized with these mothers and felt very lucky after hearing their problems; however, for practical suggestions, a group of mothers of children with dyslexia would have been a better choice for me. At first, I had hoped the parents' association of our special school might be a kind of support group, but I did not find this to be the case. However, the meetings were very helpful in obtaining information about school and after-school activities.

A mother is often advised that the best thing she can do is seek professional help as early as possible, so her child's problems do not become compounded by an emotional overlay.

While learning disabilities present a constellation of difficulties, there is no one-to-one relationship between having learning problems and having a certain set of psychological features. Nevertheless, because a child's self-esteem is often affected, psychiatric help can be very beneficial, not only for the child but also for the mother. One mother explained

> Socially, my son never had a problem outside the family, but in the family it was a living hell. He commanded the family. He had outbursts, fits. We'd run for cover. We never knew what might set it off. I literally thought he'd have a stroke or a heart attack. We'd surround him, almost wrestle him to stop. It would take hours for him to calm down. We'd spoil him, give him anything, just so he would not have a fit. It became especially bad the first year of school.
>
> We had no idea what to do, so we took him to a psychiatrist. From his first visit, he never had another fit. He was exceedingly grateful there was someone to help him handle his anger and confusion. I'd recommend professional help for anyone with more than a mild disability—for any child in special education.
>
> Philip started in first grade at age six; he still goes to the psychiatrist once a week and he's ten now. This man is perfect for Philip. He is very mild and very kind. He is also great for me. He is someone I can turn to for advice, someone in my corner. It really takes a load off my shoulders. Without outside help, I think I'd go crazy, because you do run out of patience."

Not all psychiatrists believe in therapy for learning-disabled children. Some prefer working with the parents in the belief that therapy may compound a child's perception that he is a "problem." In addition, children are still evolving and may respond well to changes in their parents' attitude.

Of the mothers I interviewed some tried therapy without success. One mother turned to it during her son's adolescence, when he seemed desperately unhappy and was taunted by his peers. Unfortunately, she reported, therapy only exacerbated the problem. She found the therapist personally difficult to deal with, although he was highly recommended. He billed her for her son's missed sessions, but never told her that her son had not kept appointments for several weeks; also, he insisted on such confidentiality that both she and her husband became afraid to talk to their son. Although a believer in psychological theories, this mother found her actual therapeutic experiences very costly and not very helpful. Interestingly, mothers I spoke with were either great advocates or strong opponents of psychiatric intervention. It seemed to depend greatly on the match between family and therapist, as well as the family's expectations for therapy.

All mothers want to protect their children from hurt. Because dyslexic children seem particularly vulnerable, their mothers may become their protectors. This can become a trap, however, as one mother explained:

> Initially, I was overdoting. It made for confrontations with my husband. I wanted to protect my son from being hurt, from feeling like he couldn't succeed. So I'd never really punish him; I'd never really make him do difficult chores.
>
> My husband would get furious. Finally, I went for counseling. The therapist explained that my husband was right. I was hurting my son by always shielding him. My therapist said, "You've never let him feel pain, but to feel competent, he must feel pain." To me, it was like watching him sink under water. I thought he would not come up again. But I had to learn to let go. It was not easy, but I could see it was better for him. It was an important lesson for me.

While we can do many things to help our children, perhaps nothing is more important than our own attitude. How a mother, indeed, the entire family, reacts is crucial. It matters less what we say ("you're great, you can do it") than what we, as mothers, really feel. Our children will sense what we feel. While I certainly know the frustrations, I truly believe there is something especially wonderful about these children. They seem more sensitive and caring than other children, but it's more than that. There is a unique lovableness and charm. "From the time I put my socks on inside out, the day went all wrong," my son told me one evening. Now I can identify with that!

All mothers want more than anything for their children to be happy. Many children with learning problems are very unhappy, and this causes their mothers great pain. Unfortunately, a mother cannot make a child happy. For children with learning difficulties, we must try to provide compensatory strategies, self-enhancing experiences, and feelings of confidence. We hope for success, but it is not entirely in our hands.

8

What Our Children
Can Teach Us

Every child is, in some ways, like every other child, yet each child is unique. Psychologists tell us children with learning problems probably feel different their whole lives. Yet, differences can also be viewed as individuality, as shown by some ten-year-old students with learning disabilities who were asked to describe themselves in terms of color.

JESSICA: *Amethyst Purple*

The color that describes me, I think, is amethyst purple. Amethyst is clear and strong, and I feel clear and strong. I also feel gentle, like a purple iris. I remember a visit with my mother to a jewelry show, where I saw a huge amethyst crystal that was so clear inside—like me.

GREGORY: *Blue*

If I had to use a color to describe my personality, I would use blue because blue is a color of happiness, and I am happy a lot. I like the Mets, and their outfits are blue. I also like blue neon. I think blue is a jazzy color—and goodness knows, I'm a jazzy person.

BEN: *Black*

If I felt sad, I would feel black. When I start to yell, it's like the world going black inside me. I feel like a terrorist is coming out of me, shouting at everyone around me. That's how I feel when I feel black.

JEREMY: *Peachy-White*

To explain me, you really would need to use a peachy-white. I think this color blends into a crowd, and I don't really stand out. I also feel happy, sad, and mad always, so this color suits all those feelings in me.

The children saw their mothers in equally rich hues. One wrote, "the color that I think describes my mom is green. My mom is gentle, like grass, but sometimes she can be mean and loud like a tree." Another child noted, "My mom's favorite color is red. Red is a color of joy, and she has lots of joy in her." Still another child said, "To best describe my mother is the color of orange. I would pick that color because she isn't one solid thing. She changes her feelings and moods."

As adults, our uniqueness and complexity bring pleasure and are prized. For children, however, being different may bring humiliation and pain. In a 1988 study published in the *Journal of Child Psychology and Psychiatry,* a six-country survey of 1,814 children in grades three through nine showed what children considered stressful in their lives. Surprisingly, children shared similar concerns even across national boundaries. For them, a fear of being humiliated far outranked many events that adults had always thought more troubling, such as the birth of a sibling. The survey also showed that school life and peer opinions played a key role in a child's self-image.

These findings are particularly interesting for mothers of learning-disabled children. "We all think we know our own children, but too often we don't really see, or hear, or understand what is really troubling them," said Kaoru Yamamoto, a psychologist at the University of Colorado School of Education, who has done important research on children's perceptions of stress.

The survey results underscored how an embarrassment or humiliation can be an especially stinging blow to a child's emerging sense of worth. Indeed, this is so significant that one of the most common triggers of suicide in children and teens is a humiliating experience. "A child's self-image is forming continually and is very shaky," comments Dr. Ann Epstein, a child psychiatrist at Harvard Medical School. "They tend to blow some things up out of all proportion. These injuries to self-esteem, in their minds, can come to define their whole identity."

All children are acute observers and measure themselves critically against their peers. If their performance is poor, they may become the object of teasing and social ostracism. But the worst damage is what they come to think of themselves; they may become losers in their own eyes. The child who does not do well comes to expect to do poorly. Research indicates such a child often attributes his failure to some unchangeable trait. Interestingly, this also impacts a child's own goals. He will often set unrealistically high or extremely low goals. Even if the low goals are met, they are so minimal that success leaves the child unsatisfied.

One of the benefits of special education classes and special schools is that these children no longer feel out of step. In such settings, certain academic difficulties are the norm rather than the exception. In reading their essays, I noticed all these children spell phonetically; all confuse *"their* and *there," "witch* and *which,"* and *"our* and *are";* all have difficulty with past irregular tenses. One fourth-grade dyslexic boy reflected feelings probably shared by many of these children, when he wrote: "A lot of the time I feel uncomfortable. I feel like nobody understands me. With the teachers, I sometimes feel like a baby rabbit about to be eaten up by twelve hungry foxes."

Despite difficulties, maintaining a sense of humor is important for mothers and children alike. At first, this was difficult for me. I was deeply worried, and I did not find the difficulties funny—I found them painful. Yet, a child can sometimes show us the brighter side.

A gifted, dyslexic fifth-grader showed he had kept his sense of humor by making the following report card on himself:

> Brice is one of the most disorganized people I have ever met.
> I will definitely help him get on the right track, if the incompe-
> tent rascal will let me.

> I suggest he move to the lower class; maybe he should go into the lower school (how about kindergarten?) and try to work himself up. He always interrupts his classmates. If he cannot control himself, he must be taken to the doctor and treated with Pepto Bismol. His ability in this class is like a paralyzed boy on a highwire, fifty feet above the ground, without a net underneath. The boy is an innocent child, but when it comes to school, he is a horned devil!

Because these children may encounter hurt and humiliation, it is important to listen to them. This advice is not as simple as it sounds. With the increasing demands on mothers today, our children may get pushed aside, without our even realizing it. I came to realize that "just a minute" and "wait a second" had become my all too familiar responses.

How much a child talks depends on the signals he receives from us, the listeners. When we listen, we convey our subconscious feelings. If our face brightens, if we smile, nod, or move slightly forward, all of these things show the child that his words are being well-received. However, if we look away, screw up our faces, scowl, or show impatience we convey negative feelings and, almost automatically, the child will cut his talk short. The truth is our feelings are visible even if we don't want them to be. Because a mother is often a child's most sympathetic and supportive listener, a child's feelings can boil up inside until there is tremendous anger, if supportive listening is not offered.

Not only must we listen but we must also strive to hear the message behind the child's words. "I hate school" might really mean "The work is hard for me; the other kids can do it and I can't." "I forgot my book" might signal "I didn't understand the assignment." "The other kids are dumb" might really mean "The kids don't like me."

Sometimes the messages are positive, but we do not realize it. Often, children seek activities that complement their weaknesses. One mother explained:

> My son signed up for crew his freshman year at college. I was not enthusiastic. I thought, what will he ever do with it, how will

he use it? I also worried that it might take badly needed time from his studies. But he was so right. It has given him an instant circle of friends and status among his peers. Most importantly, it has organized him. He's the type who wastes time; the more open the time, the more he wastes. The physical demands of crew are daily, so it has given his day a structure. I thought it was a terrible idea, but now I see how wrong I was.

Another mother told me her son chose karate. She was disappointed because she had found lifelong pleasure in tennis and believed in "social" sports. She refused to pay for his lessons, feeling karate was a foolish choice. Yet, her son pursued it. In hindsight, she realized how perfect the sport was for his needs. It taught him self-assurance and self-discipline and built up his strength. These traits were significant in his maturation from a small, tentative boy into a more disciplined, muscular, and assured adolescent.

My younger son, who was always active, decided to take drum lessons. My husband, who loves classical music, felt that almost any other instrument was more melodic; yet, the drums provided a perfect outlet for our son's excess energy and gave him much pleasure. The activity is not particularly important, but the self-esteem achieved from doing something enjoyable is crucial.

Richard Devine, a thirty-three-year-old dyslexic and an award-winning metalsmith whose works are on display at the Smithsonian Institution in Washington, D.C., explained that he had a severe speech and reading problem that had caused emotional problems throughout his childhood.

> The school system and society were telling me "You're a reject because you don't know how to read and write." I feel so fortunate to have stumbled on to woodworking, pottery, and jewelry-making—it literally turned my life around.

Today he is sharing his outstanding success with about fifty students, ages twelve to seventeen, who attend the Norman Howard School, a school for learning-disabled children in Irondequoit, New York. Six days each semester, he brings them to his home studio to make unique class rings and pursue other projects. As a result, several of these students have won citywide jewelry competitions.

When Devine approached Betsy McIsaac, director of the Norman Howard School, with this idea for an art program, he put it very simply. "What the students really needed," he said, "was a chance to succeed at something."

WHAT OUR CHILDREN ADVISE

Many special children are hypersensitive to the feelings of others. They notice immediately changes in our expressions—the unspoken message behind the spoken word. How we feel, not what we say, is what they "hear." It is our nonverbal language that impacts them. I remember my older son remarking, after his first day of first grade, "My teacher has a fake smile. I hate that."

Realizing no one could give advice on mothering better than our children, I decided to ask scores of learning-disabled children two simple things: What do you like best about your mom? What advice would you give to mothers about raising children today? Here is their advice.

GREG: *Age Nine*

I like when you ask what happened in school, because I like telling you. I like when you talk with me. I don't like when you interrupt me. I like talking.

ALLEN: *Age Eleven*

I like it when my mom says, "I'm angry. Just let me calm down. Don't talk to me," rather than starting to yell and scream. She gets annoyed a lot in her business—then it is like a gun and I'm the target, and the bullets are like anger bullets, and they hit me. This way, she doesn't take it out on me, and that is much better.

FREDERICK: *Age Eleven*

If your kid doesn't have friends in the school, don't worry. Sometimes kids can start very bad and end very good. That happened to this kid Jocelyn. Everybody hated her, but now the kids all like her. She used to squeal and the kids hated it, but she doesn't do that anymore. One day she was out sick, and everyone asked about her. So, if your kid is not doing well with friends, things do change.

JESSICA: *Age Eight*

I like when you help me with my homework when I have trouble, and I like when you listen to what I have to say.

LAWRENCE: *Age Nine*

I like when my mom is interested in the things I like to do.

MARK: *Age Twelve*

If your kid is a brat and he wants everything, don't get him everything. Tell him how you feel, and he'll tell you how he feels. You'll have a long discussion. The next thing you know, you'll love to be with him, and he won't be asking for a thing.

NINA: *Age Eleven*

What I like best about my mother is when she plays Trivial Pursuit and I am reading the question, and she helps me with the hard question, and she helps me with the hard names and big words. This is very important to an eleven-year-old who has trouble sometimes."

JOSHUA: *Age Ten*

I think mothers should express their feelings without screaming. Maybe if you don't yell, the kid won't get all frustrated and angry, and he'll just do it.

JONATHAN: *Age Nine*

Talk to your kid because, if you don't, he'll be lonely, even if you're there in the house.

GABE: *Age Eight*

I like when my mom tucks me in bed. I always sleep good when she tucks me in.

Inner-city children with learning disabilities have the problems of drugs and poverty on top of their learning struggles. When I interviewed high school special education students in the New York City public school system, their answers showed the dominance of these overwhelming social and economic concerns. Here is their advice to mothers.

JAMES: *Age Fifteen*

Stay loose.

ODESSA: *Age Fifteen*

Treat your two kids alike, not different. Stop them from hanging out late at night, on the street. Love them a lot and take them places.

MITCHELL: *Age Seventeen*

Send the kids to school every day.

GWEN: *Age Sixteen*

I'd warn them about how they do raise them. I would show them how they should talk to them. I want my children to be educated, smart people.

RICO: *Age Sixteen*

> I would send my children to a good college, even if I didn't go myself.

JANETTE: *Age Seventeen*

> My parents kept me in school for an extra year when they wanted to get rid of me. I have already agreed not to have any children.

A happy child can accomplish a great deal; an unhappy child may become overwhelmed by negative feelings. It is important, therefore, to monitor how the child is feeling. This does not mean a mother can make her child happy; the child must do this for himself, but, a mother can recognize the importance of her child's happiness.

While our children's difficulties are real, as mothers we can help them with their perspective. A child's attitude about himself is formed early and carried with him for a lifetime.

I remember one time when I was about to go to a parent-teacher conference for my ten-year-old. Fearing what I might hear, I asked, "I'm going to get pretty good reports from your teachers, right?" He hesitated, looked straight at me, and said, "I am doing my best."

Before I could comment, he continued, "Our baseball coach told us, 'I want you guys to go out there on the field. I don't care if you win; I don't care if you lose; I want each of you to do your best. That's it.' " He told me he always remembered that.

The wisdom of a child—it brought me back sharply to what's important. As my baseball-loving son so wisely put it, ". . . doing your best—that's it!"

9

A Talk with the Professionals

One of the problems of being a special mother for me was the dizzying array of professionals I had to sort through. Years ago, there was little help for these children and their parents. Today there is so much help it is bewildering.

Personally, I found myself uneasy with many of these professionals. They made me feel like I was in the hot seat. They seemed to be weighing everything I said and judging everything that went on in our family. I got the feeling that they were secretly saying to themselves, "If she didn't act this way, they wouldn't have these problems." I felt like I was being placed under a magnifying glass, and I did not like it.

Although we live in New York City, where experts abound, for us, good advice was extremely difficult to find. I mention this because, at the time, I felt it was my fault for not getting along well. After speaking with so many mothers in researching this book, however, I found upsetting experiences with professionals seemed the rule, not the exception. In my isolation, at the time, I never knew this.

Many mothers mentioned they left the professionals' offices more, rather than less, confused and upset. One mother said the doctors glibly told her there was no way they could tell, at such a young age, what was wrong with her daughter: "All too often I would hear, you'll just have to wait until she's older, wait until she begins to say her first words, wait until she begins to put words together, wait until she speaks in sentences, wait until she gets into kindergarten." She pointed out that waiting was something that just did not come naturally or easily to her. "I'm the type that is always popping the oven door open a million times to see if the cake has risen yet," she explained. It was not only her natural impatience but also a feeling that her daughter's problem could not wait; she panicked at the thought of wasting important and irretrievable years just waiting.

Although waiting was standard advice when her daughter was young, there was a period when all these problems were thought to be emotionally based. One warm, down-to-earth mother re-called how all the teachers considered her son bright, and each year they felt he would eventually catch on. But by third grade, when he was still unable to do the work, she was told his problem was emotional. A psychiatrist was recommended. After the evalu-ation, she asked the psychiatrist why her son would have emo-tional problems when her other three children were doing just great, and her mothering had been about the same with all of them. He explained that when he asked her son what animal he wanted to be, the boy said "a giraffe." The psychiatrist explained this really meant he wanted to see what she and her husband were doing in their bedroom. "He asked all these questions: 'Did you shower with him? Did he ever climb into your bed? When did you stop breastfeeding?' It was crazy," she explained. "We had just taken our son to the zoo and he loved the giraffes. Sure he climbed into our bed; we snuggled with all the kids. But what did that have to do with his reading and math? At the time, I became so confused. He was the professional; he must know, I thought."

When a child is not succeeding, parents are thrown off base. They feel confused. At a time when they need clarity they often get just the opposite.

Parents cannot do it alone, however. They need the profes-sional. One reading specialist compared her work with dyslexics to that of a dentist, explaining, "You can't fix a deeply rooted cavity by yourself but, with good dental work, you don't lose your teeth.

Despite the finest dentist, however, if you've got poor teeth, you always will and may even need more dental work. But, you'll chew; you won't have pain; and your life will be uninterrupted. Remediation is much the same."

I found the secret was not simply professional help but finding the *right* professional. When you find that person, you definitely know it. It does not have to do with degrees alone, although training is *essential,* or age, although experience helps. It is all those things and more. We found that special professional in Greg's second-grade teacher. She was young and very pretty. I used to say, "They dropped Mrs. Kaminsky from heaven just for you, Greg." That is exactly how I felt. I remember once he invited her to a play at religious school. He did not have a speaking role, and she knew that. His entire part was to hand three items to the king. Yet, she traveled a great distance one wintry Saturday evening just to attend the play. After it, she went up to him and said, "You did wonderfully. You remembered everything." He just beamed. She knew just the right words to say. Through the years, she has continued as his tutor. When I would get impatient, if he did not understand something, he would often say, "Don't worry, Mrs. Kaminsky will explain it to me." She was there for him and he knew it.

They have a great personal relationship. When I see them walking down the street after tutoring, I can just tell they really enjoy each other. But it is more than a personality match. When Greg makes an error, she seems able to zero in immediately on exactly what his confusion is and, therefore, explain it clearly to him. At one point, I remember he always confused *our* and *are.* I had asked his teacher to help him with it; I also had corrected him repeatedly with no success. Somehow, when I mentioned it to Mrs. Kaminsky, she said cheerfully, "Oh, that's a common mistake. I know what will help him." After she worked with him, the confusion stopped. A skilled professional can make a real difference.

The professionals profiled in the following pages have dealt with many of these children and their families. They speak on issues that are typically encountered by special mothers.

RESOURCE ROOM TEACHER

Martha Byne has been a resource room teacher for grades four, five, and six in the Somers, New York, public school system for the past ten years.

A resource room teacher is a teacher within the elementary or secondary school that works with children with identified special educational needs. Each child receives an Individualized Education Program (IEP) that specifies areas where extra help is needed—for example, reading (decoding or comprehension), math, spelling, and handwriting. They also teach strategies for coping with classroom assignments.

In New York State, the maximum is twenty students per resource room teacher, and the minimum time is three hours per week. For some students, it might be four forty-five-minute sessions a week. When the time exceeds 50 percent of the day, the student must be considered for a special education class.

Do Mothers Recognize There Is a Problem?

Usually, yes. New parents tend to say, "My child doesn't pay attention; he'd rather fool around. He doesn't listen." They often say, "I have difficulty working with my child." The mother becomes aware of problems when there is such resistance.

For resource room, a prime time for remediating basic skills is, I think, grades four, five, and six (ages nine to twelve). The children understand the need for instruction and they are most willing to take instruction and apply it. Later, they are more resistant; the social awareness is greater.

What Is the Biggest Difficulty for These Mothers?

The mother worries about the future. When a child is not successful in school or with his peer group, he may seek a group where he is accepted. Sometimes children resort to negative behaviors—delinquency or drugs—for attention.

What Are the Common Pitfalls for a Mother?

One common pitfall is defending the faults of their child; for example, giving excuses for unfinished homework. Mothers try to be protective, but it may make matters worse for the child.

Homework is an issue just filled with pitfalls. Mothers must be consistent. If the child asks, the mother should be there to help him with the homework. The unmotivated child becomes a tremendous problem. It could be he's afraid of failure and feels he can never meet his parents' expectations. Some children lack the attention to sit and do the homework; then you must provide breaks. A child may absolutely refuse to get the homework done; then they don't want to go to school because they know there will be consequences. In these cases, counseling is helpful. Often parents find their efforts are met with only resistance and anger. It is not easy for these mothers.

Are There Any Particular Problems
for High-Achieving Mothers?

In some instances, the parents will equate problems with their own early school experiences. They think that because they succeeded, so will their child. The child might have more serious problems but parents don't realize it. Often, this type of mother invests a lot of time and puts many demands on her child, conveying, indirectly, the need to be in the mainstream. What this does is make the child feel badly about himself. He gets the message, "I'm not good enough."

I know of one high-achieving mother whose daughter has learning disabilities. If something in school is difficult, she will keep her child home. Because of the child's problems, this mother takes charge of her life, creating an unhealthy dependency.

What Is Your Advice to Mothers?

I think accepting your child at whatever level he is and seeing him as a good person is the most important thing. He should feel, "I am lovable and capable." If parents perceive the child this way, he will also see himself this way. He will naturally drift toward a positive attitude. I would encourage mothers to help their children explore extracurricular activities—anything apart from academics. We have one student who is the fastest runner in the school; another painted a statue in town, raised rabbits, and became an eagle scout; still another is the best pitcher on the baseball team; yet another child just wrote an article about learning disabilities for the *New York Times.* All are terrific kids who gained great self-esteem.

EDUCATIONAL THERAPIST

A private educational therapist for more than twenty years in New York City, Elizabeth Cliff Horowitz, Ed.D., does educational evaluations and remedial tutoring.

It is a common misconception to think an evaluation seeks primarily to find the cause of a learning problem. Instead, an evaluation shows where intensive help might be most beneficial. The evaluation also addresses the whole picture, so a school or after-school placement can be selected with a thorough knowledge of the child's needs.

Periodic reevaluations are recommended—one in first grade, fifth, tenth, and then, perhaps, before college. A school psychologist, teacher, or pediatrician can often recommend an educational evaluator.

Are There Any General Patterns in the Mothers You See?

Certainly, some common themes emerge. Generally, there is a lot of initial anxiety. Mothers are deeply worried and wonder, "What's wrong with my child?" There is also guilt. I just tested a seven-year-old whose mother was divorced when the child was two. Through all the changes in her own life, the mother had not spent a great deal of time with the child. Now she felt immense guilt, ruminating if only she had stayed home or read to him.

In such cases, the educational evaluation helps the mother realize that, no matter what she had done, the child would still have these problems.

Usually, there is also anger. "Why did this have to happen; it's just not fair," mothers will say. I agree with them, because it is hard, and it is something that is not fair. With educational intervention, however, the mother probably will begin to see improvement. With time, most mothers come to an acceptance.

What Should a Mother Tell Her Child Before the Evaluation?

It should be something very simple. You can simply say, "You seem to be struggling with the reading and math, and we'd like to find out how we can make it easier for you." I think it is important for the mother to emphasize the help aspect.

Some mothers may fear that taking a child for educational testing will be a frightening and unpleasant experience. Although evaluations may be stressful, being at the bottom of the class day after day is very tough, too.

The typical child is scared, and I deal with it before any testing begins. I tell them I understand they are nervous. Once you talk about it, and they see you know how they are feeling, they begin to trust you, and usually are cooperative. I also start with easy tasks, to give them a feeling of confidence. Ideally, the evaluation will not undermine or discourage the child, but will provide an avenue for enhancing the child's esteem.

How Old Are the Children You Evaluate?

Usually, I see children toward the end of first grade. At that age, the children without problems learn very rapidly on their own. It becomes obvious that some children are really struggling and need to be taught everything.

If the problem centers on writing and organization, it usually becomes apparent around the third or fourth grade. At that time, the children who mastered decoding but find reading comprehension difficult are also identified.

However, if a mother herself notices a problem before formal schooling—a speech delay, markedly inarticulate speech, if the child is not speaking in sentences by age three—an early evaluation should be done.

For an older child, a poor showing on the SATs might be a reason to seek further information. Sometimes parents are afraid to have it on a school record, but today colleges are much more receptive to kids with learning differences. Once in college, the child will need some extra attention, so it is wise, in advance, to address these needs.

What Does an Educational Evaluation Cost?

A complete educational evaluation includes a parent interview, four to five hours of testing for the child (for younger children, it's done over two to three sessions), a final interview with the parents, and a written report. A private evaluation costs between $550 and $700. Usually, this is not covered by insurance. The Board of Education must provide free evaluations for all certified special education students.

What Should You Do If Your Child Does Not Like the Tutor?

If the child does not like the tutor, I think the child should go to someone else. It may simply be a bad match. However, if this happens several times, the problem needs to be explored more deeply. Most tutors find, at the beginning, there is a sort of honeymoon period in working with a new child. After a time, the child may perceive the work as "a drag," but a mother must love the child enough to be firm and insist he get the needed help. The parent should meet and interview the tutor before any remediation begins. Generally, I feel the mother should then intervene very little in the tutoring process. She can be most helpful by reading to her child and doing things that are pleasurable with him. A happy child is much easier to teach.

How Long Will a Child Require Tutoring?

Almost all parents ask me that, but I just can't predict. There are so many variables. It depends on how hard the child works, the child's internal maturation, what is going on at home, and what the teacher and curriculum are like in school. Tutoring should terminate when the child is able to keep up with the work at school, with confidence. Tutoring is usually terminated gradually.

*Is There One "Key" That Is Most Important
for These Mothers?*

I try to encourage mothers to deal with the difficulties as matter-of-factly, lovingly, and patiently as possible: to cope in a calm manner. Just as a mother would get glasses for a child's vision problem without great fuss, these children need educational and language help. If a mother is very anxious, the child may pick up this anxiety, and it will interfere with the child's learning.

●   ▪   ●

Every educator recommends educational evaluations. They are like a road map; it is tough to travel unless you know first where you are and, then, the best way to get there. One mother told me an evaluation was the best thing she did. "You learn so much. At last, I felt like I understood my child."

Having said all that, I also want to share my own personal bias. I am a terrible test-taker . . . always have been . . . so I am certain this has much to do with my thoughts. I am suspect of test scores.

When my son Mark was very young—I think around three—an evaluator gave him a test using shapes. He had to draw the shapes and then select which was the rectangle, upended, etc. Well, he didn't do just poorly; his performance was so poor his test could not even be scored. I remember feeling great pain at these test results . . . almost panic. After my meeting with the evaluator, I took a long walk by myself and then stopped at a friend's house. Seeing her child playing happily with a busy box, I remember suddenly bursting into tears.

Two years later, when Mark went to a special school for first grade, I went to the New York City Board of Education to get busing services. In order to qualify, they had to test and certify my child as learning-disabled. At the evaluation, the psychologist again told me that Mark had performed extremely poorly on this test with shapes. Among other things, he could not draw a diamond and, although he did get a score, it was in the lowest possible percentile. The evaluator looked at me soulfully. But this time, I smiled and replied, "You know what this means to me—when Mark grows up and becomes an engineer, I'm not going to walk under any of his buildings, and I don't think you should either!"

Why was my attitude so different? I think the initial news is very hard to take: it is something we don't know how to handle or make better. But by the second test, Mark was a bit older. He had learned to swim, learned to ride a bike, and learned to cross the street by himself. Teaching him these things had been tough, but he *had* learned. He was now a happier, more capable child. I realized he was going to make it, and I was going to make it, too.

After the second test, I took my son by the hand and said cheerfully, "Come on, let's get a big milk shake!" We, mothers, cannot let this testing thing get to us—and, believe me, it can. The world is a big place. There is a wonderful niche for our children and, with our help, they'll find it. Forget the scores.

EDUCATIONAL DIRECTOR, SPECIAL SCHOOL

Yvette Siegel is the educational director of the Stephen Gaynor School, a private school in New York City for children with learning disabilities. It has ninety-four students, ages five through thirteen.

How Do Mothers Handle the Stigma of a Special School?

The child is really less stigmatized by intensive remedial education than he is in a regular school, where other children may tease him. The teasing begins very early, even before kindergarten, when the clumsy child may trip over blocks. Children feel tormented when they think they cannot keep up.

In a special school, however, all learning situations are geared for success. Some parents think of remedial education as a move downward. In truth, it is not a negative but a very positive experience, enabling the child to gain self-esteem.

Will a Special School Make the Child Feel Bad?

Parents are often concerned about this. Yet, the child already knows he has a problem. Rather than feeling bad, most children feel relieved that, at last, they will get the help they need.

When Should Special Education Begin?

Clearly, all studies show the earlier the intervention, the better. Special education should start at ages three, four, or five. Today, there are educational instruments that can measure children at risk. At our school, we would not take a child unless he was at risk because he would be usurping the place of a child in need of our services.

How Is the Teaching Style at Your School
Different from That of Regular School?

We do not impose a curriculum, but begin with a child. We make him eager for learning. The unrealistic competition for an external goal does not rule either the teacher or the administration. We are concerned with the ego strength of the child, the fulfillment of his potential, whatever it may be.

For example, our children do not need to learn Greek mythology at age eleven just because someone wrote it in a syllabus. What's the use if the child cannot access the information? Instead, our approach is to have the children learn when they are ready, so they can experience the joy of it. The child is not distracted by all sorts of pressures, but is both challenged and rewarded as progress occurs.

How Does the Attitude of These Mothers
Change Over the Years?

I feel mothers become much more aware of the positive aspects of individual differences. They hold in suspicion the idea that all children must excel in the same way. They reexamine their goals and come to realize that a worthy child is much more than the sum of his achievement test scores.

Most mothers come to understand that early supportive education strengthens a child; it does not weaken him. It gives him a chance to regain his self-esteem and get an accurate perspective on his difficulties.

DIRECTOR, SPECIAL SCHOOL SUMMER PROGRAM

Tom Cone is director of the summer program at the Eagle Hill School in Greenwich, Connecticut, a six-week, half-day (8:15 A.M. to 12:15 P.M.) program for the learning-disabled child. There are eighteen teachers for the sixty youngsters, ages six through thirteen. The students take four classes daily: literature, writing workshop, math, and a one-hour, two-to-one tutorial. There is no homework.

When Should a Mother Consider a Summer School Program?
It should be done in collaboration with the professionals working with the child. Sometimes a mother wishes to keep it a secret from the school; however, we need school records to design the best program and placement for each child.

What Is the Best Age or School Year for Summer Intervention?
The younger the better. As children get older, they tend to get more defensive. An older child may ask, "What is the message here? Why are they sending me to these small classes during the summer? Maybe I'm not as good as I think I am." However, for a first- or second-grader, none of that even enters their minds.

How Do Summer Students Compare with Your Year-Round Students?
Our summer students have better skills and have made a better adjustment to traditional education. Of course, virtually all of these students have experienced difficulty in school; all are getting additional help, either outside tutoring, resource room, or psycho-educational therapy. Their disabilities are milder and less pervasive. Their needs are more specific. The whole design of our program is different. We are preparing these students for where they are going in September. This is a short-term, intensive program to fill specific, academic holes.

Why Should a Mother Consider a Summer School Program
Rather Than a Special Camp That Offers Daily Tutoring?

I believe if you need academic help on a remedial level, it is a
school-related problem and should be dealt with in a school setting. These children do not shift gears well. It is very difficult for
them to come out of a pool or run off the tennis court to a math
tutor. Much precious time is wasted in their emotional transition;
real learning is sacrificed.

Here, we don't ask the children to make changes. At eight-
fifteen, they know they arrive at school, ready for school. There is
a consistency of expectation. They work in the morning and then
all afternoon they can play.

What If a Child Vigorously Objects to Going to Summer School?

A decision such as attending summer school, is not a shared
decision. It is a parent's responsibility. We had two children this
year who were screaming and saying they hated their mothers, and
refusing to come. Parenting is not always easy, but parents must
prioritize and stick to difficult decisions.

To help parents deal with this resistance, both parents should
be equally strong in their commitment. Too often, the mother
takes the full impact of a child's resistance. This is not just difficult
for the mother; it is not good for the child. It is also important for
a mother to get input from teachers and support staff, so if the
child resists, a mother can be sure of the importance of the program. In our experience, the children who try the program stick
with it.

With Such Success, Do Many Children Come
for Several Summers?

A small percentage do come back. However, if subsequent summers are needed, it would be a clear signal that the child's current
school may not be the best place for that child. Success here provides an insight for parents into the difference a correct placement
can make. An honest evaluation of the child's needs and schooling,
rather than repeated summer programs, is our goal.

What Is the Cost?

For the six-week, half-day program, the cost is $1,200. It is tax-deductible for parents of students with documented disabilities. Some large corporations have employee benefit programs that may provide stipends toward this cost.

• ■ •

Greg attended the Eagle Hill summer program when he was eleven and about to be mainstreamed. I thought the program was excellent. One mother who had just moved from the south and had been told only recently of her son's learning disability said she was disappointed. She felt these experts would get to the source of the problem and spend the summer fixing it, so that her son could really soar during the next school year. Instead, she found "just school." Of course, there were smaller classes, excellent teachers, and explicit explanations, but still notebooks and worksheets—"just school."

I knew exactly what she meant, but having been through it before, I realized there is no quick cure. I felt the program was immeasurably better than private tutoring, an alternative I had seriously considered. Motivation was easier because all the children were working. I got the feeling that the four hours passed quickly for them.

To me, one of the best things about the teaching at Eagle Hill was the way everything was broken down, step by step, in a clever way. For example, one of the writing assignments was to get yourself stuck somewhere—a factory, a museum, a store—have an adventure, and then, somehow, escape and present a moral. (My son got himself stuck in a spaghetti factory in Washington, D.C., spent his time swimming in tomato sauce and throwing meatballs at the president, and escaped by throwing down a long rope of spaghetti. His moral: if you're going to a food factory, take a fork!) In a creative but concrete manner, the lesson taught the children organization: beginning, middle, end, and conclusion.

To be honest, I worried what the other children would be like. Such worry turned out to be absolutely groundless because they were a lovely group. The students were so nice in fact, I hoped for more friendships, but there were few social opportunities—no lunch, gym, or school functions.

No child welcomes school in the summer, and my son did complain at times. I felt particularly bad when he remarked one morning, "I will always remember I had to go to summer school." It made me wonder about the message I was conveying.

● ▪ ●

In his insightful book *Children at Risk,* Gary A. Cross states, "The first maxim for those concerned with children is to give a maximum effort and involvement." He believes that for difficulties involving children, it is always better to become overinvolved or to overrespond than to be underinvolved or to underrespond. "While you risk being accused of exaggerating a problem, you should never underestimate the real seriousness of a child's difficulties."

Professional help, whether in the resource room, special school setting, private tutoring, or summertime remediation, does not come without sacrifice for both parent and child. Parents must live with both the expense and the child's resistance. The child gives up the pleasure of carefree time

While we want and need professional help for our child, we also, let's be honest, deeply resent it. These professionals are often the bearer of news we do not want to hear. Their very presence reminds us of a difficulty most of us would rather forget. We may inappropriately displace our frustration and anger onto the messenger rather than the message.

I remember feeling great anger at the professionals when my children were young. Although I did not express these feelings, I am sure my feelings were not so hidden. At the beginning I hated the special school: I hated its name; I hated walking in the door. I hated that I had to be there; I hated that my sons had to be there. I hated the teachers who were, I thought, moving too slowly; I hated the homework which I thought (or was it hoped?) was too easy. I was very impatient with the problem. Looking back now, I am immensely grateful for the basic skills and organizational techniques these professionals taught my children. I am grateful for the motivation they helped instill. Most of all, I am grateful to them for overlooking my anger and trying to do what was best for my sons.

10

Grandparents and Friends: Support but Sometimes Stress

Undoubtedly, you have already heard one of the following:

- He's just a slow starter. Be patient.
- He's just young. It's immaturity.
- This is a lovely, sweet child—I don't know what you're talking about.
- If you didn't live in the city and take him to all those fancy doctors, he'd be in a regular school doing just fine.
- Is all of that really necessary? Sounds like some newfangled educational mumbo jumbo to me. Are you sure you're not overreacting?
- There is nothing wrong with him. He's just a spoiled kid, too much TV. You're not strict enough with him.
- It must be from his father's (mother's) family. No one in *our* family ever had such problems.
- Please don't tell anyone. They won't understand; they'll think he's retarded.

These are common reactions of grandparents. As learning problems stress the immediate family, they also have implications for grandparents.

In general, the women I spoke with said their own mothers were supportive. One woman recalled, "My mother could zero in on my daughter's strengths, but she could clearly see there were problems there. She could recognize it." Another mother commented, "My mother could not be more supportive. She is someone to talk to, to complain to. She listens and sympathizes. She is concerned, along with me, on a day-to-day basis." Yet another told me, "My parents did not really understand, but they said, 'Whatever you think, we know you are doing what's best.' "

Usually, women who already had difficulty with a mother or mother-in-law found that the stress of having a dyslexic child worsened the situation. My relationship with my mother-in-law was uncomfortable because she operated within a strong denial system. She asked me not to tell her family of the children's problems. They were her relatives and I wanted to respect her feelings, yet such hiding brought me feelings of shame that I did not like.

In conducting the interviews for this book, however, I saw that my mother-in-law's reaction was a very common one. The mother of a seven-year-old dyslexic boy told me:

> My mother-in-law thinks nothing is wrong—it's all in my imagination. She thinks a problem means there is something wrong with her, so she doesn't want to acknowledge it, and she blames me. She feels I've created it from my background, and it is not really so. My mother, who was a widow for years, was a bit of a hypochondriac, so she says this is my pattern. But, she never discusses it. She refuses to. My husband told her there might be a genetic factor. She got incensed and said, "Absolutely not." Frankly, I'm resentful.
>
> We have financial pressures from all my son's occupational therapy, speech therapy, and tutoring. He went to a therapeutic nursery school that was very expensive. Given the situation, I think she should help us out, at least a bit. But she feels these things are unnecessary, and she does not want to hear about them or pay for them.

Another mother said her mother-in-law seemed to try very hard, but was just not on her daughter's wavelength.

"My daughter had an awful time in school. She despised it, yet the first thing my mother-in-law always asked was 'How's school?' Sacha would say 'good,' 'fine,' 'yes.' Rather than taking the hint and seeing her obvious resistance, my mother-in-law would say how important it was to apply herself, to get her homework done, and really work at it."

Perhaps grandparents need to deny for their own emotional reasons, but such an attitude leaves a mother feeling totally unsupported. When people negate problems, the problems do not disappear as wished. Instead, this denial distances people. This feeling of distance and isolation comes at just the moment a mother needs support most. This inevitably causes deep resentment.

In too many cases, a grandparent may be unsupportive of a learning-disabled grandchild. One fifty-year-old interior designer, who is the mother of an adopted fourteen-year-old boy with learning difficulties, explained:

> There is lots of blame that goes back and forth. It is all mixed together with my mother-in-law. We have another adopted child—a girl, Jane. She's a child who would make anyone proud. She's very brilliant, pretty, popular, wonderful, and she always has been. When we went to adopt a second child, my mother-in-law would say over and over, "Don't do it. It will just be trouble." We were supposed to get a baby, but something happened at the last minute, and it didn't come through. After that, my mother-in-law started saying even more, "Why don't you forget it?" She said she had two children and is close to only one. She kept saying that my daughter is so great; anything after her would be terrible. It planted doubts. And, of course, when problems with my son started—almost from the outset— all of this preyed on my mind.
>
> For years, my mother-in-law had promised to pay for the children's schooling, but after she saw John's poor school work, she did not want to pay. She said, "Why can't he go to public school? It's money down the drain." Once I found an excellent special school that he loved. But it was very expensive. I just could not swing it. So, I went to her and asked. But she turned me down flat.
>
> I talked to her twelve ways to Sunday. I'd say, "John is not backward. His mind just goes faster than his words. He can't get it out fast enough." Well, she paid lip service to it all, but forget it. I could tell she didn't believe it. What's worse, she acted like he was backward. Believe me, he knew it.
>
> Jane was her favorite. She made absolutely no effort to hide it. She'd invite Jane to stay with her and not John. She always invited Jane to come and stay with her for Christmas vacation,

from the time my daughter was ten. When John turned ten, he said, "Grandma, Jane came when she was ten; can I come now?" But she said no flat out. She told me he ran around too much; he'd upset things. It hurt him. So, I said to her, "I can't allow this; you are hurting him." She said, "I'm not hurting him. Don't I always send him a present?" She refused to see how hurtful she was.

Just as we have fantasy children, we also harbor fantasies about grandparents. My image of the ideal grandmother has always been that twinkling fairy godmother in Cinderella. A friend of mine says she longs for the ever-patient, all-accepting grandmother in Edna Le Shan's books. For both of us, reality in no way resembles fantasy. My friend, whose oldest child has a serious reading difficulty, feels her mother is not a good grandmother. "She gets her roles confused. Because she knows I've had trouble with my son, she tries to protect me, tries to make things better for me by disciplining him. But he resents it and he balks. They get into escalating conflicts."

Being a grandparent is a complex task; sometimes our parents are not sure just how much to be involved, when to say something and when to keep silent. One mother of a fifteen-year-old dyslexic boy told me, "This is a second marriage for me, but Jerry is my son. My new husband and I are both very strict about sticking to our word with Jerry. I remember one incident that happened years ago. We were eating at my parents' and my husband said, 'Jerry, you have to sit at the table until everyone is done.' But Jerry was finished and wanted to play with his cars. Nevertheless, my husband firmly forced him to stay. My father, a kind and gentle man, told me years later that it just made him cringe. Now that Jerry is in a regular school and doing well, my father told me we were right: the strict limits worked. Things are smoother now, but with learning disabilities, family relations are always a bit bumpier."

ONE GRANDMOTHER WHO HAS MADE IT WORK

Woodruff's grandmother has a magic way with children. I remember one Saturday morning when she came to our house and proclaimed, "Come on boys, we're all going ice skating for Woody's birthday." Before she came, I had tried to convince them to go out, but my efforts had been met with only whining and resistance. Her energized approach had them out the door in two minutes. When I went to the rink to pick them up, everyone, including Grandma, was on skates and flushed with enthusiasm.

My son loves going with Woody's grandmother. When she picks the boys up at school, she always has a snack for them—bread, fruit, or granola bars. It is a simple thing, but my son looks forward to it. Because she is so well liked, I asked her how she manages it.

In the beginning, Woody's dyslexia was such a problem for me. I am a schoolteacher by profession. I was having great trouble rethinking my ideas on how people learn. I couldn't think in alternative patterns. I kept thinking more of the same will help, but it was not working, and I was becoming angry and frustrated.

We met with a psychologist at his nursery school. It was very, very helpful. Now I know it sometimes takes counting to twenty, when counting to ten has always been hard for me. They taught me to say, in a positive way, what I might just instinctively have said in a negative way. It is that old philosophy of seeing the glass half-full. They also advised us not to teach him, and to make home a safe, comfortable place.

Woody has always been a lovable child, and this made his dyslexia even more hurtful. At the same time, it eased things. It was not difficult to see that he really does have more positives than negatives.

Today, at almost age ten, after three years of special school and three years of one-to-one tutoring twice a week, Woody still reads on a first- to second-grade level. But his comprehension is at the level of age thirteen. He made a poster the other day that said "DRUGS KILL," but he spelled *KILL, KLLI.* I thought this simple word showed it all—somehow his brain just switches things.

When I'm talking about it to my understanding friends, I still have to work on concentrating on the positives. If you dwell too much on the problem, it is just destructive to everyone, but I can't help thinking how hard it will be for him all the way up the ladder.

I don't dwell on the "it's not fair" factor because, at my age,

I know about life. I look around at my friends who have much worse problems. I'm going to a memorial service today for a friend's son, who spent the last six years fighting cancer. I have friends whose very bright children—children who had everything going for them—have gotten into drugs or run away. I'm thankful that, at my age, I still can't take anything off my taxes for medical bills, and I'm very lucky to be nearby my grandchildren.

Woody and I have always had a close relationship. I think one of the best things I've done is read to him. We read absolutely everywhere—on the bus, waiting for the tutor, in the park, in the coffee shop, even outside when he's playing quietly. I always have a book in my shoulder bag. Sometimes he'll be playing and he'll say, "Read to me, Grandma, I can hear you." He's ten now, and he still loves being read to. Once you get started, the children really get hooked. It is also wonderful for me. I'm not very good at playing games, but I love reading. So, we both enjoy it. Sometimes Woody will say, "Remember that book . . . read it over to me."

These days, I try to approach things differently because of Woody. He has really taught me a lot. I am very capable, but I may run over people getting to my goal. I'm always on time. Woody's approach to time is unfathomable to me. He can't tell time—he can do it somewhat with a digital watch—but he doesn't always wear his watch. Through him, these days, I'm learning to enjoy the process and not just the goal.

My latest idea is to have his phone number and his dad's office number laminated onto his key chain. It's a problem because he can't remember phone numbers and, if he's late, I get worried. This way, he can just take out his keys and he'll always have it with him.

These children are under a great deal of pressure, even though they don't always show it. We wanted to arrange for some tutoring during Woody's stay at overnight camp this summer, but he just screamed, "No! No!" His intensity made me realize the pressure he must feel. The psychologist had a good compromise. He suggested we forget the tutoring and give him a crash course two weeks before school starts, but it's constantly a juggling act for us.

One mother told me her in-laws did not understand the difficulties at all, but she never tried or wanted to explain them. By simply being there and loving her children, she felt they were doing exactly what grandparents should.

Because grandparents are members of a different generation, most mothers turn to their friends for support. Generally, they do this with mixed success.

WHAT WE CAN—AND CANNOT—EXPECT FROM FRIENDS

"Mothers wear their children on their sleeve around this town," one mother remarked. "A smart and accomplished child is the ultimate status symbol."

There is undeniably a feeling that a child is a reflection of his parents, but even more a reflection of his mother. In Betty Osman's book *No One to Play With,* she describes the pain of a learning disabled child's social struggle. I believe there are social effects for special mothers, too.

I knew mothers who mumbled the name of the special school, when speaking with casual acquaintances, almost in embarrassment. I never felt that way, but I did begin to feel uncomfortable when people I hardly knew would ask, "Exactly what is his learning disability?" I did not want to discuss my child's difficulties with people I hardly knew or even with those I knew well. I found it hard to say the right thing that would sound cordial, not curt; supportive, yet not Pollyannaish.

One woman whose eighteen-year-old son is an outstanding swimmer and a member of the high school football team, but is also very dyslexic, explained:

> I get annoyed at my friends. I don't want them to look down on my child or categorize him as stupid—even if they don't come right out and say it.
>
> I have one friend who's very competitive. Because all her children have excelled, anything less than an Ivy League college is simply unacceptable to her. She pays lip service, but she looks down on my son. Her attitude is patronizing and condescending. If I do say something, which I often do, I'll say,

openly, "You know, there is no equivalency between IQ and
how a child performs in school," she'll say, "Oh, I didn't mean
it that way!" but I can feel her attitude. Sometimes, if there are
three mothers together, she'll turn to the mother of a high
achiever and just exclude me. All of a sudden, it's like I'm not
there.

Sometimes I tell her, you know, John is strong in areas where
Jason isn't. Sometimes this is the only thing that gets to her, and
she'll say, "You're right," but the next day, she forgets all about
it and is back to her status game.

This woman explained that, with most friends, she is very forth-
right about what a learning disability really means, but sometimes
she feels she's hitting a brick wall, and then she just changes the
topic.

Mothers often find certain stages with friends more difficult than
others. For me, nursery school was awful. Perhaps it was because
I, myself, was never comfortable in nursery school. Psychiatrists
say that if a mother found a particular passage difficult in her own
life, she is bound to find that time problematic in her child's life
as well.

Many mothers find the last year in high school particularly
stressful because the next step needs to be planned. The academic
level seems to determine everything. There is much overt compar-
ing among mothers; in fact, it seems the only topic of conversation
the entire year. After immense effort and years of tutoring, it can
be emotionally battering for both mother and child to be relegated
to second choices.

"I'm very open about it," one mother of a high school senior
explained. "If I weren't, I'd be saying I was ashamed. I don't need
to make excuses. I am very happy and proud of my son."

My husband, like most fathers, did not get as emotionally em-
broiled. He just did not experience stress among friends as I did.
This brought me a needed perspective. I had a college friend who
would talk endlessly about her very talented daughter. Being with
her left me filled with tension. When I confessed this to my husband, he said I was overreacting and, as a friend, she should not

have to watch her words. His opinion made me take a second look at my feelings. I realized, at times, I did tend to take this talk too personally and to be overly sensitive.

Although a few old friendships were stressed, I met some truly extraordinary new friends among the other special parents. Many of these parents have done remarkable work, not just for their child, but in reaching out to others. They have turned a difficult situation into a very positive one.

I met several mothers who became special education teachers. One wonderful father, a lawyer, said his son's needs made him so interested in the field, he now volunteers one day a month doing mediation, going to court as a child advocate, and helping parents obtain the special services and financial aid their children need.

Many parents have become leaders in dyslexia societies. Perhaps outstanding among them is Carrie Rozelle, whose own struggle with her three dyslexic sons led her to establish The Foundation for Children with Learning Disabilities, (now called the National Center for Learning Disabilities). Iris Spano, a warm and inspiring woman who is the mother of a dyslexic son now in his thirties, was among the founders of the New York chapter of the Orton Dyslexia Society. A past president of that chapter, Dr. Stanley Antonoff, a dentist, is the father of four dyslexic boys. Through their difficulties, he discovered, as an adult, that he had learning disabilities. His activism led to the establishment of a program at New York University Dental School for dyslexic students, as well as extended-time benefits for students taking Dental Achievement Test.

Anne Schneider realized the need for more extensive university-level services when her hard-working, learning-disabled daughter floundered during her freshman year. She has dedicated herself to developing a broader spectrum of support services at Boston University. It is her hope that these support services will inspire other universities to upgrade, reevaluate, or perhaps even initiate similar services.

When I interviewed parents for this book, I found a warm camaraderie. We commiserated together and laughed together. One mother told me she dropped off her son at college for his freshman year and received a call from the college dean even before she could unpack her suitcases. Laughing, she said that she had expected problems, but this was a new record for speed!

Friends, new and old, can help mothers through the most stressful times. My friends confirmed for me that I was not the awful person I sometimes felt I was becoming. While I knew all the "right" attitudes, I yelled way too much and became much too angry when working with my sons on their homework. My most helpful friend told me she did all these terrible things, too; just hearing that made me feel better.

When family and friends are supportive and seem truly to care, it is joyous to share happy occasions with them. At my older son's bar mitzvah, his performance was outstanding, and my joy unbounded. For me, after all the special schooling and early difficulties, sharing this joy with those who had also shared the struggle seemed to have a depth and special feeling one could almost touch.

11

Facing the Finances: Fitting Costs into the Family Budget

Having a child with learning difficulties is not only an emotional stress but a major financial one as well. The costs of special schooling, tutoring, and various therapies are staggering. In families where money is already an area of disagreement, these expenses can further stress relations, as one divorced mother told me.

> My husband and I were both very concerned about our daughter. He was supportive in terms of her education. I cannot take that from him. But my husband's reaction was "What will it cost me?" This was his reaction, however, to *everything* . . . everything in the marriage, everything in the divorce, even after. My reaction was "How will I make this work?" But the costs of Gwen's special school and tutoring were tremendous. It affected all of us. We had two other children. Money became an even bigger issue in our marriage. The disagreements increased.

"If I didn't have to pay for special school and tutoring, we could take vacations," the mother of a nine-year-old boy commented. "But I feel I have no choice. He desperately needs it." The mother of an only child remarked, "My husband and I tried to have another child. Unfortunately, it never happened. We fully expected to have these same problems again, but we figured we could muddle through emotionally. Financially, now that was the real question."

While most remediation services are tax-deductible, few are covered by medical insurance. Costs rise each year. The following figures were compiled for 1988 and probably are now slightly higher, but this will give parents approximate budgeting figures.

- *Diagnostic Centers.* Learning disabilities diagnostic centers charge on a sliding scale from $200 to $900 for a full evaluation, including parent interviews, a battery of psychological and educational tests, and a conference interpreting the results. At these facilities, a parent should ask in advance the total cost and be sure a written evaluation is included.
- *Special School.* In areas of our country, where public school programs are inadequate or overcrowded, there may be a need for a special private school. In New York City, the two elementary schools for learning-disabled children have annual tuitions of $12,500 and $14,700. One does not accept public funding. A private secondary school for children with learning disabilities in New York City has an annual tuition of $13,400.
- *Special Boarding School.* Throughout the country, there are boarding schools for learning-disabled high school students. At the Landmark School, one of the most highly respected, the tuition is around $21,600, varying slightly depending on the specific program selected. Landmark, like many boarding schools, also offers a seven-week summer program designed for high-potential dyslexic high school graduates and college students. It costs $4,500.
- *Private Tutoring.* Unquestionably, the most basic service almost all these students receive is tutoring. Private tutoring costs about $40 to $80 an hour and is often needed for years. Because this involves large sums, the whole field of tutoring is booming. There is much possibility for exploitation: anyone can call himself a "learning specialist," so a mother must be wary and check both qualifications and references. Educators say if no improvement is observed within eight months, parents should switch tutors.

Most insurance companies do not reimburse tutoring services. A few policies offered only to employees of certain large

corporations may cover tutoring if it meets certain requirements, however. They will cover services done by a "licensed"
professional, for example, a licensed psychologist. They do
not cover educational specialists, however, even those with a
Ph.D. because these professionals are not licensed. They may
cover services done at a licensed learning center or hospital-
affiliated center. Since policies vary, it is important to check
your own.

- *Speech and Language Therapy.* In most cases, this therapy is
  recommended at least twice a week. Language specialists say
  that if this therapy is done only once a week it usually takes
  much longer to be effective and, therefore, in the end, the cost
  will be greater. At a hospital clinic, there is a sliding scale,
  depending on one's financial situation. In the top bracket
  (family incomes more than $50,000) the cost is $75 per session.

- *Eye Exercises/Coordination.* For eye exercises to be effective in
  changing eye-movement patterns, therapy is needed once or
  twice a week for eight months or more (time required depends
  on the specific condition). Once-a-week treatments average
  $175 per month. For families with major medical insurance,
  many policies cover 80 percent of reasonable charges.

- *Psychotherapy.* These children may encounter emotional problems related to poor self-image and difficult peer relations, so
  psychotherapy may be recommended once or twice a week. At
  the beginning of psychotherapy, a therapist often makes a
  point of stressing that therapy will take a long time. If behavior
  problems are involved, it may take even longer. After one year
  of weekly visits, it is possible that change will not yet be apparent, even with excellent therapy. However, when change does
  occur it is long-lasting. The cost is between $60 and $120 per
  session, depending on where you live and whether a psychiatrist, psychologist, or social worker is used.

  Because the child's problems are so intricately interwoven
  in the family fabric, some therapists will not work with a child
  unless the parents also receive therapy. Family therapy generally costs between $70 and $130 per session.

- *Special Day and Overnight Camps.* There are camps for learning-disabled children that provide close counselor/camper ratios, generally one to three. These range in cost, but may run higher than comparable regular programs (sometimes they cost the same but have a six-week rather than a seven-week session).
- *College Support Services.* Private institutions usually charge a fee in addition to tuition for support services. The fees vary depending on the type of support offered. On average, they cost $2,000 to $3,000 per year in addition to tuition. Publicly funded two- or four-year colleges do not charge extra fees for support services.

How can parents pay these staggering bills? How can divorced mothers, already financially squeezed, manage financially? How can special families take the vacations they need to renew themselves and keep their perspective? How can parents possibly afford it all?

Obviously, choices must be made, but this is not easy. Tutoring and psychotherapy produce long-term results, but are very difficult to evaluate in the short term. Knowing what to sacrifice is never clear; therefore, establishing priorities is anxiety-provoking and guilt-producing.

Many women must earn the money for their children's services on their own. Studies show that almost half of all children under the age of eighteen are living in households headed by single parents (usually women). Government studies show that one in three women lack even the basic skills to earn a reasonable living; however, these expenses demand good financial resources.

For a single mother, not only present finances but also the financial future of herself and her child are concerns. "To be honest, I'm worried John's problems will be a strike against me," confessed one divorced mother of a learning-disabled boy now thirteen. "Sure, it's great to say I would not want a man who did not care about my son, but, the truth is, men today are calculating and there are plenty of women out there. A man may look at all the expenses and problems and just say, 'No way.'"

In the struggle to cover costs, parents must work long hours, which often produces stress. Stress is not just uncomfortable but, according to David Elkins, professor of child study at Tufts University, it produces self-centeredness, leaving little strength or enthusiasm for parenting. However, a lawyer who is the mother of three, two of whom are in special school, told me this is not her reaction at all. "After dealing with all the aggravations at work—we are moving our office and one of my key assistants just quit—I can't wait to walk in the door and be with my kids. It's not a chore; it's a relief."

What are we getting for our hard work and money? "My husband calls it paying our dues," one mother of three, whose oldest son has learning disabilities, remarked. "So much has been just thrown away—no long-term changes, no real progress but, for ourselves, we had to feel we've left no stone unturned."

Many parents feel they pay high taxes for education and, therefore, it is a school's responsibility to take care of a child's learning problem. While this is logical, reality is far different. Mothers must seek appropriate services and then monitor progress closely. "You've got to stay on top of things," many mothers told me.

The greatest financial help is the Education for All Handicapped Children Act, (PL 94-142). This legislation, passed by Congress in 1975, provides free and appropriate education for all handicapped persons ages three to twenty-one. Learning disabilities were recognized by Congress as one of the handicapping conditions requiring appropriate education. It is an eligibility-for-all law meaning it is not based upon the economic status of the family. This important feature made it clear that *all* children are entitled to receive services enabling them to achieve their potential. The law states that special programs must be provided to enable a child to achieve his or her potential and, if such programs do not exist in the public school system, then the government must pay private facilities to do the job.

However, there is a shortage of funds because of the vast number of students who have evidence of learning disabilities. To qualify for aid, the child must receive an evaluation through the public school system. To obtain funding for private school, a parent must prove that the public school cannot provide for the child's needs.

This is done at a Board of Education due-process hearing. To represent the parents at this hearing, a knowledgeable lawyer is advisable. While parents are entitled to represent themselves, the legislative regulations and endless red tape make this unwise. Even if the parent is competent and knowledgeable, the calm detachment of a professional may be more effective, especially in view of the fact that the school board will have its own attorneys present.

The process is strained and anxiety-ridden, but the outcome is crucial in terms of dollars and services for the child.

For the high school graduate, the state vocational rehabilitation office is a place parents may find some funding. Your child must be registered to qualify and although this means more red tape, it is worthwhile. To be eligible for services, a student must have both a disability that is a handicap to employment and potential for employment as a result of rehabilitation. Although this funding is usually not major, it may provide some portion of tuition expenses, or pay for tutors or note takers. Funding varies from state to state; often these offices are more willing to pay for in-state services.

The Internal Revenue Service considers a learning disability a condition that may qualify for medical deductions; therefore, the following services may be tax-deductible:

- Tutoring
- Occupational therapy
- Special schooling
- Transportation to and from special schools
- Room and board at a residential school
- Special camps

To deduct the costs of a special school under section 213 of PL 94-142, the IRS requires that a doctor recommend the need for such schooling, that the child's learning disability be certified, and that the special school meet certain defined regulations. Remember, the deduction of transportation charges in connection with tutoring, as well as the tuition cost of the special school is allowed.

Unfortunately, income tax deductions are less valuable than they once were because of the 1986 Tax Reform Act. With lowered tax rates, the value of a deduction has diminished. In the upper brackets, one saves only twenty-eight cents rather than fifty cents for each dollar spent. Effectively, this increases the cost of services for a learning disabled child.

The new tax act also affects when these medical deductions begin. Previously, medical costs were deductible when those costs exceeded 5 percent of the taxpayer's adjusted gross income. Now, those costs are not deductible until they reach 7.5 percent of the adjusted gross. In effect, this again increases the cost of services to our children.

The new tax law increased the tax exemption for each child to $1,950; however, for a parent to claim an exemption for a child over five years old, the child must have a social security number. With the new tax law, children are no longer automatically in a lower tax bracket. With the imposition of the "kiddie tax", if the net unearned income for children under age fourteen exceeds $500, the income is taxable. When it becomes taxable, it will be taxed at the parents' rate. Unquestionably, the new tax law has deeply affected special families, increasing significantly the financial burden.

Estate planning is also important for parents. This planning is done to eliminate taxes involved in passing one generation's assets to the next. Many of these financial aspects seemed complex to me (I'm sure it was my math disability!). The one very important thing I have learned is EVERY PARENT OF EVERY CHILD MUST HAVE A WILL. A will allows a person to determine exactly what will happen to his assets after his death. If there is no will, the person dies intestate, and the state will decide what will happen to the funds.

A will can be changed as the needs of the child become better understood. In most states, when an individual turns eighteen, he becomes an adult and is presumed to be competent to handle money on his own. Some learning-disabled children may not be ready to assume this responsibility at age eighteen, however. One common solution is to leave the estate "in trust" for the child. This means a trustee is appointed to manage and conserve the estate; he then pays the child a set amount of income regularly.

Of course, no tax filing or estate planning should be done without the advice of a knowledgeable financial professional. Expert advice is mandatory in this highly technical area.

To help us make the best use of our money now, I asked mothers what, dollar-for-dollar, were the most beneficial services for their children. One felt the best-spent money was for her son's drum and guitar lessons. These greatly enhanced his self-esteem. Another mother mentioned her best-spent money was for a wonderful outward-bound-type weekend course her son took when he was in junior high. These teenagers spent the weekend away, learning survival skills. They did mountain climbing, rock climbing, spelunking, camping, and even spent a weekend learning to survive with little money in New York City. The environmental experiences gave him feelings of confidence that really changed his feelings about himself. He knew he could not just survive: for the first time, he could also do things many of his peers could not.

Through the years, I have come to realize that, while you cannot buy a cure (indeed, there is no cure), early educational services are the best investment a parent can make. In our criminal courts we see lost, learning-disabled children, who were either never diagnosed or, if diagnosed, never received adequate help in the public school system. In New York City, probation officials estimate that as many as 40 percent of the city's 14,000 youngsters in family court are learning-disabled. More than 60 percent of adult prisoners are thought to have learning disabilities, and many believe the figure is even higher. Children with undiagnosed or untreated disabilities are more likely to get into trouble as they are unskilled, suffer from low self-esteem, and can be swayed easily by others.

Most of these children receive no services because they come from families where parents, often uneducated themselves, are working poor or welfare recipients unfamiliar with learning disabilities. Yet even for concerned parents the financial obstacles might be overwhelming.

A recent study in the Brooklyn family court found about 27 percent of the children identified as learning-disabled came from families that did not qualify for Medicaid, but they were too poor to pay for tutoring sessions in private centers.

Too many children are on a financial wheel, which almost inevitably spins them to failure and crime. Their spinning is not in a vacuum. It is costing all of us.

Judge Jeffrey H. Gallet, a New York State family court judge who is himself dyslexic, has been working to have taxpayer money used for educational services rather than court costs. "We do almost nothing for these kids," he stated. "Helping them is expensive, but not as expensive as court costs. An acquittal costs ten thousand dollars in my court. If there is a conviction and probation, the costs rise to thirty thousand dollars. For forty thousand dollars we can help eighty, maybe a hundred kids."

Judge Gallet has been active in getting services for these children because, as he put it, "Almost every week, I see a learning-disabled child who, undiagnosed or untreated, is venting his or her frustrations in antisocial ways. I could have stood in that same spot. If not for loving, caring, involved parents, my frustrations at not being able to keep up in class and, to some extent, in the play yard, could have burst forth in the same self-destructive way."

Even for children who receive the best early treatment, the struggle continues into adult life. While as mothers we worry about paying for services, by far our main concern is how our children will manage financially in their own lives. The world is highly competitive; competence is required. You cannot expect a boss to be supportive and understanding.

The story of Debbie, a long-haired and pretty twenty-four-year old, shows how academic struggles can translate years later into career concerns. One week after Debbie's wedding to a construction worker, I spoke with her mother.

> Debbie is just beginning a job as a nanny, taking care of a four-year-old and six-year-old and doing some light housekeeping. She'll come riding over on her bike, a bandana in her hair, the music blasting, the kids in tow, and the dog yelping alongside. It's vintage Debbie. Of course, I worry about her future, but at least she's happy today and I have not always had that.

After high school, Debbie took a two-year equestrian program. It was only the end of the first semester when she came home and said, "I'm wasting my time and your money." With the practical courses she was great, but as soon as the academic side came, she did not want to do it.

Of course, I was disappointed. I felt it was important for her financial future, and also for her feelings about herself. But I knew if she didn't want it, I could not force things. Even without a degree, she did work for a local vet, but it lasted only six months. She has strong feelings about how animals should be treated, and when something was less than perfect, she let them know, loud and clear!

Then she worked for a while with a local housecleaning service. She made good money, but she had a hard time when people knew us; it was embarrassing. There is a part of her with high aspirations, so she did not handle it well.

She worked for a short time as a salesperson. This was more socially acceptable, but she found it sterile, uninteresting. She's very active and did not like the feeling of being tied down. Once she worked and lived at a stable, but she had some friends who tended to hang around, and that soon ended.

Debbie met her husband through a dating service. Basically, she said she was looking for someone macho and much older. I think, in her heart, she wanted someone to take care of her. Jeff was none of these things. . . . He's six-four, slim, blond, sensitive, and just her age, but I feel it worked because they have so much in common. He is also adopted and he did not enjoy school either. They seem wonderfully comfortable with each other.

They both have a lot of growing and maturing to do, but I feel they will do it better together than apart. My husband and I have spoken to them jointly and told them we are willing to help them out if they want to go back to school. Debbie listened and didn't actively respond, but even that was a sign of increasing maturity. Her usual response to any suggestion before was "Mom, I'll do it my own way, in my own time." Now that they are married, I don't want to give as much guidance. I want to pull back.

I've been there calling the shots for so long; I think my daughter has a lot of resentment. "Why did you send me to that camp with all those jerky kids?" she'll ask. I think the motivation of their marriage and starting a family will do more than my suggestions, anyway. Now, it's their time. Ideally, we'll be offering emotional support but, on their part, there must be a recognition that it's up to them.

How can we make our child's financial future brighter? One mother whose son is going to a special college program this fall feels, more than anything, that she wants her son to get a college degree. She explained that he had been accepted at a more competitive college and her husband had wanted him to go. His philosophy, she explained, was that their son should go to the best possible place. However, she was afraid that he might become overwhelmed and drop out. She had learned job skills on her various jobs and assumed he could do the same, but she felt that "piece of paper" was crucial to his financial future.

In the fascinating way of so many aspects of life, one mother explained how her son ended up earning much of his college money through his greatest weakness: dysgraphia. His writing was so completely illegible that she knew it would be a major stumbling block throughout his life. In his technical high school, she asked that he be given a typing course. There was a computer-typing program in the regular high school, but they would not offer it to the technical students unless this mother could find a group of six students. She did, and it worked out well for all of them, but especially for her son. He became so skilled, he typed college term papers and earned a great deal of his college tuition!

As mothers we want to make life easier for our children and do not want them to taste defeat and hurt, but we cannot live for them. As the mother of a twenty-five-year-old put it, "I can only suggest; he's got to do it."

12

After High School, What?

"I took my son's high school diploma and put it in our safe-deposit box," one mother laughingly confessed. "I knew we could never do it again." Just as parents are delighted and relieved, they must gear up for a whole new set of decisions.

After high school, the choices are wide-ranging. More than anything, we want to place our children on the proper path. We do not want them to flounder. But knowing what is best is not easy.

"I was seized with terror," one mother admitted. "From the time Josh was very young, I remember feeling worried every time I had to place him in a new situation, wondering if I had made the right choice, if I had done what was best for him. But after high school it was different. I had serious doubts. What if I had been seeing Josh all these years through rose-colored glasses. What if by sheer force of will and personality I had sold everyone a bill of goods on just how capable Josh really was. Because my husband and I had gone to college, and all of his friends were going, he wanted to go, too. But should he? I was suddenly very unsure. I feared the detailed admission process was going to unmask him; he was going to be found out. I not only worried could he do it; I seriously wondered should he do it. Was I doing it only so I would look good?"

Such thoughts go through a mother's mind; not always through but, sometimes, stuck in a replay position. It is a time when reality confronts us. It feels almost like a slap that says, "Look at me, not at fantasies, wishes, and dreams. Look at me."

The transition is also difficult for students. They are deeply worried that no college will want them and concerned that if they get in, they won't be able to stay in. Because post–high school alternatives are complex, it is suggested that parents start researching possibilities in their child's sophomore year, much earlier than for other children. Basically, there are the following choices:

- Four-year colleges
- Junior colleges
- Community colleges
- Vocational and technical schools
- Technical institutions and trade schools
- Post–high school programs

None of these may be right, though. One mother said her daughter was exhausted from the entire effort of years of schooling and tutoring. She felt that the summer was not enough time to recover and wanted a year off.

> Starting in the tenth grade, she began to really find the going rough. She wanted a release. She didn't want to be tutored one minute more. I told her, "Look, your experience has not been like everyone else's up to now, so we can do this differently, too." But I didn't want her to just hang around, so we structured a year that turned out to be absolutely marvelous.
>
> First, she went to Israel with a youth group. After that, she lived with a family in Jerusalem and worked at a museum doing cataloging. Then, she spent a month working on a kibbutz.
>
> When she came home at Christmas, she got a job at Saks for the holiday season. Believe me, it was not easy. She had to learn twenty-two different procedures on the computer. I was really fearful about how it would go. She has auditory-processing problems, and all I could think of was with all the noise on the main floor she won't be able to hear and won't be able to use the machines. Everyone will be yelling at her, and she'll get fired. The first day she went off to work I was so nervous. But she came home and said, "You didn't even come to visit me." So, the next day I said, "We'll have lunch." Before we met, I

stood behind a column for a while, just watching. It was hard
for her; I could see it. But she didn't get fired; she did it. Then
she took a word processing course and a reading improvement
course at a nearby community college. When the year was
done, she was really ready to be a full-time student.

Regardless of interim measures, eventually goals and a program
must be selected. Choosing the right program for each child's
needs is crucial because an unstructured program, or one the
student cannot handle, may end in disaster. The mother of a graduating high school senior who wants to manage a restaurant but
has poor organizational skills explained what can happen when
these children become overwhelmed. "Some become withdrawn.
They spend hours in front of a TV set. Others retreat into their
homes, where they don't have to compete in the outside world."

Unfortunately, some learning-disabled students find school simply unbearable and do not want to continue. While we like to think
that good teaching always works, the reality is that a significant
number of learning-disabled students—even some who have had
the benefit of excellent special services—just do not succeed at
school. For those who do not want or cannot afford to continue
schooling, this is a time of entering the work force. Experts working with these entry-level applicants often advise them to seek
work at a large corporation where there are free job-training programs. Working while availing themselves of these programs may
increase their marketability and feelings of self-esteem.

Students who do not enjoy confined academic settings often find
great reward and satisfaction in active police and fire-fighting
work. Air-conditioning, heating, plumbing, electrical work, auto
body repair, beauty culture, horticulture, and landscaping are
other popular ten-month technical courses. The culinary arts can
be extremely satisfying for those who discover a talent in this area.

There is a vast network of community colleges offering two-year
degrees. Most community colleges have open admission policies,
which make it possible for students over eighteen to attend, even
if they do not have a high school diploma.

Junior colleges present unconventional but intriguing alternatives. One pretty girl who loved to ski went to Colorado Mountain College in Glenwood Springs, Colorado, a small, two-year school, where she became fascinated with a course in the installation of solar components in older homes. (The school also offers courses in operating ski centers, managing ski resorts, and marketing sports equipment.) She now skis, works in a friend's business, and is enthusiastic about her life-style and her work.

Another student who was an animal lover attended the New Jersey School of Dog Grooming in Madison, New Jersey. During the one-year course (an abridged, eleven-week course is also available), he learned all aspects of dog and cat grooming in a hands-on environment. It gave him just the background he needed to work in a grooming salon, with hopes of one day opening his own pet shop.

Different course combinations are often used, depending on interest and need. For example, one student graduated from a chef's school, then attended a precollege program for dyslexics to work on language and organizational skills, and finally graduated from a state college with a degree in restaurant and hotel management.

Can my child attend college? Despite a recognition of learning disabilities, most parents still dream of sending their child to college. Years ago, these students were discouraged from attending; it was felt college meant only failure and frustration. In the last decade, this attitude, as well as available college-level programs, has changed dramatically.

Today, 25,000 students with learning disabilities are enrolling in college each year. Almost 8 percent of all freshmen now describe themselves as learning-disabled.

Nonetheless, college is definitely not the right choice for all students. College admissions officers warn that many of the learning-disabled students now applying to college do not have the potential for success. Some characteristics colleges are seeking in applicants include:

- Average or above-average ability
- Reasoning skills adequate for college-level work

- Enough high school courses in the mainstream to have a broad fund of background information
- Awareness of one's own learning disability and a knowledge of compensatory strategies
- Assertiveness and an ability to be a self-advocate
- Lastly but probably foremost, the motivation to succeed—the willingness to put in the hard work, long hours, and extra effort that will be required.

Once college becomes the goal, the first stumbling block is getting in. It was suggested to one mother that, since no one knew her daughter better than she did, she should write a letter of recommendation for her. At first, she thought this might look too self-serving, but after further consideration, she decided to do it. I would like to share her letter with you.

To Whom It May Concern:

As the parents of a child who has learning disabilities, this becomes the year of letting go . . . twelfth grade and the search for the right college begins.

The past eighteen years have been spent fighting for a correct diagnosis, figuring out when to start speech therapy, insisting on mainstreaming, struggling with schools to understand that learning-disabled means "different" not "stupid," finding the right support at the right times (testing and evaluations for Andrea, guidance, both practical and psychological for us), and last, but never least—tutors, tutors, tutors.

Without doubt, Andrea's learning disabilities would have disheartened and defeated anyone less determined than our daughter. She has been an inspiration to our family and to all who know her. No one, including us, can understand where she keeps finding the inner will to meet each new problem with such steadfastness and equanimity. It is ironic that the one thing that causes her the most difficulty is the thing she loves most: she loves to learn. History has become her favorite and best subject. Andrea works hard, eagerly meeting the challenge of new and complex material, but she does it with a remarkable spirit—often she can be heard singing somewhere between her sixth and seventh hour of homework.

Her academic perseverance has meant giving up many activities—extracurricular school activities, outside interests, and "just hanging out." We don't want to give the impression that she never has any fun; she loves shopping, discos, her hour of "General Hospital," and the companionship of close friends. Andrea is also an able artist. She paints sensitive watercolors, her sculpture is strong, and her weaving is intricate and expressive.

We believe Andrea is now clearly ready for the challenge and rigors of college. Her skills and grades, won with superhuman effort, have steadily improved (this fall, her grades have been almost all *A*'s and *B*'s). Because her study habits are exemplary, planning, spacing, and completing all her assignments on time, she is succeeding. Andrea recognizes that she still has certain gaps and some limitations, but she feels confident that it will be at the university level where she will excel far beyond what she has already accomplished.

Some have said, "Why does she kill herself? She should be satisfied." If you knew Andrea, you would be able to picture her getting that very determined look, a wistful smile, and saying, "Listen, I've got a lot more to do. It may take a little longer to get through—but I'll do it!"

Thank you for your consideration of our daughter's application.

Sincerely,

I spent some time with Andrea's mother to find out what happened after she sent her very moving letter. She explained that while her daughter is attending a large university, there have been problems. She had to change from the general studies to the metropolitan (evening) division, tutoring had to be reworked because peer-tutoring was neither reliable nor adequate, and she even had to take a leave one semester. But now she is a sophomore, pulling the best grades of her entire academic career, and moving toward her degree. What was this mother's advice to other mothers? Without hesitation, she said, "Stay involved. I had totally overintellectualized the process. I thought I'd be sending the wrong message if I stayed involved. I thought I'd be telling her she could not make it on her own. I had read articles that said this is the time for a parent to let go. It made sense to me. But my daughter just spun her wheels and fell hopelessly behind. When I saw the situation, we had a serious talk. I asked her, 'Do I have your permission to help you advocate?' She said yes, and I could see the relief. I had always been there for her, and now I got back in the process. I gave her the clear message, 'I'm still here for you. I want to share what you are feeling.' You cannot abandon them. They still need you."

This does not mean we should baby these young adults. One mother who insisted that her homesick son stay at college during freshman year found that this forced him to make the adjustment. Our active support will not make them dependent; just the opposite will occur: it will enable them to become independent.

There are gifted, learning disabled students at top universities across the country. Even Brown University, one of the most academically competitive and prestigious, has a large and active student dyslexia society. They formed a self-help group and even published a pamphlet, *Being Dyslexic at Brown.* Students of average ability, however, have an even greater struggle. By the end of the first semester, many find themselves already on academic probation and, after the first year, a large group have dropped out or have been asked to leave.

Studies show that ability alone is not the problem. Rather, the question the student should ask is not "Can I do the work" but "Will I make myself do the work?" Learning-disabled students usually have to work harder and longer hours to achieve the same or lower grades than non-learning-disabled students. It requires a tremendous effort. For most students who drop out, it is this effort they have not put forth.

The issue of motivation is complex. Some mothers complain that their children do not even exert average effort. One mother described her son's "laziness" as feeling like "pushing a heavy burden up a hill, with its weight pressing down on me in the opposite direction." What appears to be "laziness" may instead be the fact that so much of their energy has gone into maintaining their egos, that they have little left for compensatory work. Interestingly, a small proportion of these students go to the other extreme and become workaholics. Because one college student seemed almost unable to stop working, his mother urged him to schedule leisure activities, just as he did academic assignments.

While we usually think of college as an immediate post–high school option, some students find more success when they are a bit older. Dr. Charles Drake, founder of Landmark College, the only college in the country exclusively for dyslexic students, and himself a dyslexic, believes it is never too late to learn basic language skills. "We believe students can be taught at any age—in fact, they're better in their twenties because they've matured and can see the importance of sitting in there and grinding. Those that have survived to that point are choice people. They know what life is all about, and they know they have to work."

Because college is a time when mothers need specific how-to information, here's a brief summary of advice from various mothers, as well as from Mrs. Myrna Miller, a college adviser. Mrs. Miller, the learning specialist at Tenafly High School in New Jersey, has been guiding high school seniors for more than twenty years and is the author of *The Next Step: Post-High Paths for the Learning Disabled.*

On Disclosure

MOTHER: Look them in the eye and be honest. Don't try to talk your way in. What you want to know is will your child flourish there. If the college doesn't want to hear the needs, it is probably not the place for your child.

ADVISER: I want to stress that the most important thing is getting a student into a school where he or she can experience success, not just get in. Some schools do regard disclosure negatively; others see a learning disability as an explanation for erratic grades. Indeed, if the administration is aware of the difficulty, they may even advocate for admission on the child's behalf. I recommend calling the school you are interested in and speaking to someone in the admissions office. This is what I do for parents. It is the best way to get the most accurate, up-to-date information.

On the Dreaded SATs

MOTHER: Our son insisted on taking them like everyone else. I tried to tell him that as bright as we knew he was, he just couldn't do that. I didn't win that argument. He took them three times— timed, extended, and, finally, untimed, with the English portion read to him. His scores went from 250 and 235 to final scores of 450 and 465.

ADVISER: Take the untimed tests if you feel the grade will be significantly higher than on the timed test. The PSAT, given under regular conditions, will help you gauge what to do. The schools may look at the untimed test differently, so it can be a disadvantage. Untimed law and dental boards are now offered for students applying to graduate schools.

On Choosing a Major

ADVISER: I strongly recommend a broad liberal arts major. My thinking on this has changed significantly over the years. I used to stress specific majors, in areas of the child's strengths. But I discovered there was a common pitfall . . . the narrower the major, the more restricted the requirements. The students often encountered one or two courses they just could not get through. Changing majors then required additional courses. The broadest possible major, with the fewest requirements, is best; they can minor in their area of interest.

On Credits

MOTHER: Our son is taking three courses, rather than four, for twelve credits, but he is finding even that extremely tough. He works constantly. Each summer, he takes one summer school course at a college near our home. That seems to be working well. However, another mother mentioned her son's summer school course was condensed and moved very rapidly, making it extremely difficult.

ADVISER: Most students do take a reduced load; many require more than four years to graduate. An adviser from the learning disabilities program may be able to help the student choose a good mix of courses, so there is not an overload of required reading and written papers. They may also suggest certain professors, who are sensitive to special needs. Some colleges offer advanced summer registration to avoid overwhelming these students, with long lines and red tape.

Foreign language requirements can often be waived if a student can document his disability. Even Harvard College will waive its foreign language requirement. At Barnard College, students are allowed to substitute two years of French culture for French language.

On Special Programs

MOTHER: He has been in the mainstream since third grade, so I didn't want to take him out now. Also, the world is mainstream and he must learn to live in the real world. I did, however, select a small college, where I felt there was more individual attention, and the faculty was understanding.

ADVISER: More than 250 colleges and universities now offer support programs for learning-disabled students. They vary widely in the degree of support they provide. Some offer tutoring, counseling, accommodation services; others have a complete program with an entirely separate admissions procedure. The needs of the student determine which type of support is best.

Many parents assume admission to separate programs is automatic, but this is not so. At Adelphi University on Long Island, for example, last year there were two hundred applicants for fifty places.

Support means not a watered-down curriculum, but assistance in achieving a standardized goal. Most students in a learning-disabilities program meet regularly with a tutor. Many students spoke glowingly about their tutors and identified them as the most important aspect of the learning-disabilities program. However, tutors vary so it is important for parents to inquire—some are simply graduate students, others are trained teachers. Many students, because of auditory processing or grapho-motor difficulties, find taking notes during lectures exceedingly laborious. A note-taker—a good student who takes notes on a special noncarbon duplicating paper—may be arranged. This procedure is also used for deaf students. (Paper can be ordered from the Rochester Institute of Technology Bookstore, in Rochester, New York.) Some schools arrange self-help groups where students can gain support from each other and share helpful suggestions. Counseling—group or individual, done by a psychologist or social worker—may also be part of a special program.

Colleges are seeking students who understand their own disability and can be active advocates in arranging their own services.

On Money

MOTHER: I set up a checking account for her in her senior year of high school, so she could get used to it. It took practice.

MOTHER: I tried a checking account, but he kept loaning money to friends. Now, we send him twenty-five dollars a week in cash. It controls things.

ADVISER: Special programs can cost two to three thousand dollars additional. Extensive information on government-sponsored financial aid programs for postsecondary learning-disabled students can be obtained from the Health Resource Center, 1 DuPont Circle, Washington, D.C. 20036. If family resources are not sufficient to cover all costs, you should also inquire at the college's financial aid office.

On Roommates

MOTHER: The first roommate was not at all appropriate. He changed on his own. During the summer, he completed a profile, but the college never matched him, really. I think they just filled rooms. Now it's fine, but it does not seem as significant as I thought.

MOTHER: His roommate was the single most important thing that happened to him. He is with a boy who is organized and they study on the same schedule. He also got him active in soccer. The roommate turned out to be the secret of my son's success.

MOTHER: One does not want all learning-disabled children put together, but it's been tough. First, she was put in with three roommates. The room was a converted lounge and soon became a hangout. It was impossible for her to study. Now she changed to one roommate, but the girl is out every night and my daughter has to study. It's not easy.

On the Best Advice

MOTHER: Don't assume anything. When we first applied, we met the most wonderful woman, who was director of handicapped services. What we did not realize was, by the time our daughter arrived, she had left her position and not been replaced. It was only six months later, but so much had changed. Ask for details and plan ahead. Get as many things in place from the beginning as possible.

ADVISER: I call in parents and counsel them to get their children good supportive services. Many of these students find that, as they get into the junior and senior years of high school, they are managing well without tutoring. They think of their learning problems as over—something they had when they were young. College demands complex, analytic thinking and good time-management skills, traditional weaknesses of learning-disabled students. Many students, even those at the most prestigious colleges like Brown University, spoke of the need for some educational support. It is important to get this help *before* problems arise. I tell students, PLAN EARLY: DON'T WAIT UNTIL YOU ARE FAILING TO ASK FOR SERVICES.

Regardless of the type of support, a word processor is essential. My students tell me it is the single most important instrument in helping them succeed at college.

All children have a consistency. Their style in approaching life and facing new challenges is deeply ingrained. They are themselves. They bring their strengths, weaknesses, and personalities with them to college, and after. No magic wand is waved after high school.

One very stylish young woman with dyslexia, now a college graduate, had hoped her struggle was finally over. But on her first job, an exciting opportunity at an innovative design concern, she had great difficulty getting all her work done. Her mother explained:

> My daughter came to me and said, "I don't know what to do. I have so many back orders to fill. That is why I was hired. But all day, the phone rings, and my boss asks me to do things. It's a nine to five job, and all my friends leave right at five o'clock. But I never get the back orders done." So, I was very honest. I said, "Didn't you always have to spend longer on your homework than all your friends? If you work slower, this does not change, regardless of all the degrees in your pocket." I told her, "It goes back to expectations. It probably will take you longer, but if you don't stay, what is going to happen?" So, she's staying. It's not easy, but I think it is rewarding. They like her, and although it's demanding, she's enjoying it.

"Don't paint a panacea," one mother of a grown son urged me when I told her about this book. "It is going to be hard, and they should know it will take longer." It is important for us to be honest with our children. This will help them understand what they must do to get where they wish to go. The journey is lifelong.

13

A Look at the Future

To begin this chapter, I wanted a success story: something to show that a mother's struggle, as well as a child's, were rewarded. I had been told of a blond, pretty, twenty-three-year-old girl, who recently moved to California. She has many friends, a job she likes as an assistant at a top designer's showroom, and her own apartment. When I spoke with this young woman's mother, however, she poignantly reminded me there are, indeed, great successes (she feels that her daughter's living on her own and working are great successes), but there are no miracles.

> I am extremely proud of Kim. She's dealing with her problem and it really is very tough. You need to communicate very honestly with your child. Most important, you must be very honest with yourself.
>
> Often a mother will see certain strengths in her child. She'll see a part that works well, and then she'll blow these traits out of proportion (the "so-he'll-be-a-terrific-artist" type of thinking). You cannot give yourself, or them, inflated hopes, because you are both going to lose anyway. In the end, mothers still want perfect children. Deep in our hearts, we still want things better for them. You must deal with the reality. This is a lifelong problem—it is a monkey that is never off her back. It is always there. It's a life sentence. I know she's damn angry about it, and I am angry, too. It's rotten and unfair. On her job, there were a lot of things she had trouble with, so Kim went for tutoring. She just adored her tutor, and they had a marvelous relation-

ship. Kim felt her tutor was the first person who really understood what she was going through. But the tutor told me that Kim may need tutoring for the rest of her life. That just blows my mind. She's been in tutoring since the first grade.

If a child with this type of problem can become a self-sufficient, happy adult, it is a tremendous success. For a parent, this is a damn difficult thing to find out. But for the child, it is immeasurably more difficult, because it is always there. My daughter must navigate the world. There are no special allowances for her difficulties.

I am extremely proud of Kim. Success, yes, absolutely. Easy, never . . . not for me, not for her. In fact, she just called from California today. She met a nice guy at her health club. Kim is pretty and caring. Socially, she has her likes; she wants to do the choosing. She doesn't want to be with just anyone. Well, finally, he came over and said "hi," but she confessed she is extremely shy and she just couldn't think of anything to talk about.

So, we talked about it. I try to keep the lines open. Kim is very private about her world. We laugh. Yet, as a mother, I still ache. I still struggle along with her.

In the last few years, experts have come to recognize that learning disabilities are not outgrown. But, depending on the child's intelligence, the degree of disability, and the amount of individualized educational help, the child can achieve a satisfying life and do very well indeed. Today, there are an estimated 5 to 10 million learning-disabled adults in all walks of life.

For mothers and children, it is well to remember that very famous people have had similar difficulties. My sons thought it was terrific that Cher, Bruce Jenner, and Tom Cruise all share their difficulties. One girl in my son's class, who had trouble remembering her summer telephone number, was thrilled to hear Cher say, "Numbers and I have absolutely no relationship. I can dial a phone okay, as long as it's not long distance."

My sons' special school had successful graduates come back and speak with the children. On hearing one recent graduate, a twenty-five-year-old stockbroker, speak of his success and wealth, one nine-year-old boy raised his hand and asked, "Did you marry your wife for her money?" He had concluded this was the only way for such a student to achieve success!

Many people with learning problems have not only overcome, but excelled. Some often-cited examples include:

Woodrow Wilson. Biographers state that he did not learn his letters until he was nine, and did not learn to read until he was eleven. Letters from relatives termed him "backward" and "dull," and expressed sorrow for his parents.

Albert Einstein. Einstein reportedly did not talk until he was four and did not read until he was nine. His teachers saw him as "mentally slow" and "unsociable."

Thomas Edison. A well-known dyslexic, Thomas Edison wrote in his diary, as an adult, "I remember I used never to be able to get along at school. I was always at the foot of the class. . . . My father thought I was stupid, and I almost decided I was a dunce."

Auguste Rodin. The famous sculptor was described by teachers as "the worst pupil in school," and by his family as "an idiot" and "uneducable."

Henry Brooks Adams. The historian and Harvard graduate had such tremendous trouble with reading and spelling that his parents took him to a family physician to ask whether a blow to the head by a cricket ball could possibly account for the youngster's inability. The parents never expected him to be able to go to college.

Although historical role models are inspiring, my children were more fascinated by today's heroes. Olympic diver Greg Louganis is a perfect example. The story of Greg Louganis, an adopted child with learning disabilities, reads like a made-for-Hollywood movie, but it is true. When he began school, he was laughed at and made fun of because of a shyness caused by a combination of stuttering, speech delay, and dyslexia.

Today, at age twenty-eight, Greg Louganis is the world's greatest diver, with an outstanding record of achievement: three Olympic gold medals (a record), forty-seven national titles, six World Championships, six Pan Am gold medals, and twelve Olympic

Festival gold medals. Upon receiving a special Olympic Spirit award, he was asked what his message was to young people. "Anything's possible," he said simply. This is indeed his remarkable legacy.

Just as most children don't grow up to be Olympic champions, neither do most children with learning disabilities. What a parent can realistically strive for is a satisfying life. This is, indeed, the challenge of us all.

When thinking about the future, mothers are warned to keep their expectations believable and real. Children internalize parents' expectations, so what we convey is extremely important. If our expectations are unrealistic, we mothers will meet inevitable disappointment; what's worse, our children will become disappointed in themselves.

A thirty-six-year-old successful bank executive, who is herself dyslexic, is now seeing the future in her six-year-old daughter. When she herself was growing up, no one acknowledged her difficulties, but named or not, she remembers the hurt.

> I remember reading as a painful experience, just the visual contact with the page was, for me, painful. I went to a public school and a few teachers gave me *A*'s for effort, but I just could not do the reading. I could not answer those questions at the end of the chapter . . .

But, she also remembers the pleasures:

> My mother took us everywhere: concerts, ballet, museums. We did it together as a family and I really loved that, but the exposure was extremely important. I saw, I heard them discussing things. That's how I learned. School was just a jumble of confusion.

Despite her own difficulties, this mother still finds her daughter's problems anxiety-provoking.

> Here I am a mother with these problems and I know they're hereditary. I see things already, and I just hope we will be able

to resolve it, and the school will have the resources to motivate her so she compensates. But it's very scary.

She's a bit of a space cadet. I began to see it at age three. She's just different; her attitude toward play is noticeably different than that of the other children. It makes me nervous.

When she's not doing things up to my expectations, I get frustrated. I have to hold myself back. I know it's a fine line and, if you don't handle it right, there can be big trouble. I know she's different, and I tell myself to sit back and enjoy the differences. But it doesn't come naturally. I have to make a big effort. When I'm not doing it, though, I remember my mother's rigid way and I know that's disastrous. She's a sweet child, and I worry she'll blend into the woodwork.

To me, these problems are a matter of time and gut. I think the key is getting the children so excited about the end product, so interested, that they are willing to suffer. Children must be excited and motivated; otherwise, they just close the door. If they are motivated and interested, they'll put in the hard work, and it is harder than for others—but they'll overcome, they'll get there.

Over and over, educators and mothers credited perseverance as the one trait, more than any other, that brings success. Successful learning-disabled children demonstrate perseverance from an early age. They were able to stick with the difficult task of learning, even with minimal gains at times.

One thirty-four-year-old physical therapist explained, "I didn't fail, but that was because I almost killed myself trying. I had a simple formula for success—if I wanted to do as well as the next person, all I had to do was work twice as long and twice as hard."

A successful businessman, who graduated from Vassar College, but also graduated from an elementary school for children with learning disabilities, believes, "If you can make it through elementary school and high school, you can make it through anything!"

Perseverance takes real grit. To understand the struggle of these children, one mother recalled how she returned to college at age fifty-four. The first day, the instructor rattled off all sorts of complex instructions. Suddenly, she became so utterly confused and overwhelmed, she felt almost in a panic. Listening to this experience at the dinner table that evening, her daughter, without missing a beat, responded, "That's how I feel every day of my life."

While all children worry about measuring up to their peers, the psychological suffering of learning-disabled children is definitely more complex. "It seems that learning disabilities always result to a greater or lesser extent in moments of helplessness, confusion, and, as a result, feelings of humiliation and failure," explained Dr. Jonathan Cohen of the psychological counseling service at Columbia University in New York City. "In fact, many learning-disabled children and adolescents evidence a tendency toward panic anxiety. In other words, when they become anxious, for whatever reason, a sense of panic rapidly ensues."

Dr. Cohen noted that even in the seemingly best situations, where parents and teachers respond in a supportive and empathetic fashion, the children are still plagued by these psychological complexities.

For most students, indeed, most people, perseverance is possible for only so long without success. A fascinating recent study of elementary school students in Maryland found that the lowest-achieving elementary school students spent more time with homework than students with better grades.

Yet in junior high and high school, low-achieving students devoted *less* time to homework than high achievers. Dr. Joyce Epstein, the author of this study and a professor at the Center for Research on Elementary and Middle School at Johns Hopkins University in Baltimore, Maryland, has said, "The slower elementary students are willing to spend extra time on their homework because they still feel there is hope for them to succeed in school. But by the time high school comes around, many simply see no point in continuing to do what they're not successful at."

In urging perseverance, mothers must not only build in success but also acknowledge the courage it takes to persevere. The tremendous importance of "wanting it" and perseverance is demonstrated in the moving story of a severely learning-disabled young man.

During elementary school and junior high, his mother was deeply worried about her son's future. She honestly felt he would not be able to graduate from high school, and she would have to set up some sort of trust fund.

After graduating from the alternative high school, he wanted to go to college. Her husband, a waiter, was dubious, although he was a strong believer in education. The young man's school advisers said, "No way, out of the question." His mother was not sure herself that it was a good idea, but after discussing it at length, both she and her husband decided that if their son wanted it so much, they owed him "the chance to fail."

They found a small two-year college with a resource center. His mother recalls, "His high school record was absolutely awful. When they accepted him, they took a risk. He's one of those kids who has no snap or crackle . . . somehow he always looks like he's lounging. But I think they saw what we saw—he wanted it and he was willing to work." This young man not only graduated but transferred to a four-year college from which he will graduate at the end of the year with a degree in therapeutic recreation. During the summer he worked at a residential drug rehabilitation center in Vermont and was so well liked by both patients and staff that he was offered a full-time job after graduation.

There is great joy in seeing a child who has struggled succeed, but the path to success is never easy. This young man complained of stomach cramps at times, a symptom his mother feels was the result of the stress such effort produces.

Part of being a mother is reliving the feelings of childhood. One mother confessed, "When I was younger, I never wanted children, and one of the strongest and sharpest reasons was that my own mother had died, and I did not want to have children who would one day feel what I had felt then."

Watching your child brings alive again in a mother old feelings from her own childhood. I remember, when my children were very young, feeling with frightening force, myself as both mother and child. As I urged my son to enjoy nursery school, which I myself hated, I felt sucked into an emotional maelstrom, suddenly thrust back to childhood, with all the painful hurt and awkwardness; yet, at the same time, I was now the mother repeating the role with my own child. I felt hit on all sides: past, present; mother, child; hurt, hope; all interwoven together like a tangled ball of yarn.

Seeing your child's pain reawakens long-repressed pain of our own. The feelings can be powerful, as one mother recalled:

> In all the turmoil with our son was the feeling, "Oh, dear God, please don't make Josh like me." I had two of the deepest, darkest secrets. I was very bright, but I really knew I was very stupid. It was my inner secret. I felt his problems were proof-positive of my own deepest inadequacies.

While a mother's emotions are intense, we must be suspect of overanalysis and too many fancy labels.

Dyslexia is just an attempt to say, in Greek, that an individual can't read. Siegfried Engelmann, an expert in the field, once said, when asked what he thought about dyslexia, "Dyslexia: I call it disteachia." He felt the "problem" was not in how the child learns, but in how he was taught. Basically, it boils down to the fact that if a child is finding learning a struggle—whatever the cause—he needs clear, organized, explicit teaching. Unquestionably, children with learning disabilities progress less easily, but they *do* learn, they *can* succeed. It is up to us, their mothers, to give them the courage to keep working at it.

One psychologist told me educational evaluation results are a bit like fingerprints; they don't change. A mother confided that she had had her son evaluated before kindergarten and again at age twelve. To her amazement, the results were identical.

In my experience, test scores may not change, but children change enormously. I clearly remember walking my son down our street to nursery school and feeling deeply worried about how this child would ever earn a living. I'd go through different occupations in my mind and then reject each as impossible. People told me not to think of the future, but this was my child forever. How could I not think of it? Lawrence Greene, who has worked with learning-disabled students for more than seventeen years, and is the author of *Learning Disabilities and Your Child,* has written, "Despite the fact a learning-disabled child may be only six years old, doors to potential careers and professions are already beginning to close. Unless his learning problems are resolved, these may ultimately reduce the child's future potential earning capacity by as much as 75 percent."

Today, with the benefit of early special education, my children have changed in ways I would have thought impossible ten years ago. Mark, who could not hit a ball, is now a B+ranked tennis player. Greg, who we were told absolutely needed "tracking" therapy because he could not catch a ball thrown directly to him, is now an excellent first baseman and finds his greatest pleasure in playing baseball. They are both in regular school and doing well.

That is not to say that difficulties magically disappear. They both must work hard at school. But both boys are happy and motivated, which makes any difficulties so much easier to handle.

For this book, many mothers shared family photo albums to give me a better idea of their children. One mother told me you could chronicle her son's stages—the happy years and those of great discomfort—by the expression on his face. As a mother, I knew exactly what she meant. Looking through our albums, I can see not only their expressions but my own. To me, the rocky periods are apparent in tension on my face, and the ease and happiness of seeing them, at last, progress and thrive, is apparent there, too.

"There are, however, residuals," one mother of a dyslexic son, who is now a successful stockbroker, explained. "Many of these children never own their success; rather, they consider it an accident, just luck. Because of this view, they see the bomb around the corner . . . something about to come and sweep it all away."

The mother who told me this is a competent, esteemed community leader. She then admitted that she recognized these feelings because she is dyslexic, too. She said that when her son became successful, he was more receptive to talking about his problems. As he talked, she recognized many of her own feelings that her success was just luck, that others would discover she was really a fraud.

She felt we must educate our children so that they "own" their success. Although all people have insecurities, she felt adult dyslexics grapple with this ever-threatening failure more than others. A mother cannot eliminate all the hurts of growing up, but a child's understanding and awareness can build inner strengths.

To me, no one is more important to a learning-disabled child than his or her mother. As Doreen Kironick, an author and also a mother of two learning-disabled children, has stated, "No one else will hurt quite so much over his disappointments and defeats, and no one else will be quite as choked with happiness over his achievements and joy."

This does not mean that we mothers can make our children successes. The idea of blaming a mother for a child's failure is cruel. A mother cannot determine how her child will turn out. She does not have that much power.

Louise Bates Ames, Ph.D., founder of the Gesell Institute of Child Development at Yale University, explains, "A child is the kind of child he is because, to a large extent, he was born that way. How you treat a child can have a strong influence on the way he turns out and will, very likely, determine whether or not he is able to express his best and finest potential. But, in the long run, it is the child's inherited potentials, rather than the way you treat him, which make him the kind of person he is."

For a mother, learning disabilities often translate into anger and frustration. Most mothers find the intensity of their feelings embarrassing, guilt-producing, and confusing. But there are positives about all of this. Such feelings are the thing that spurs a mother to seek help. It is one of the goals of this book to show the commonality of difficulties, but also the importance of moving on—of focusing on the child's strengths and abilities.

I remember attending a dyslexic society conference, where all sorts of experts were expounding on complex theories of brain hemispheres, reporting advanced optical and auditory findings, and explaining innovative educational gimmicks. An elderly psychologist rose and said, "By now, the mothers here must be totally befuddled about what is the right path, what is the answer. You know the one I'd put my money on? I'd bet on the mother. Mothers know their children like no one else. The mother who fights for her child, who is there for the child, and who encourages the child will have the child who thrives. Despite all the breakthroughs, and they are exciting and important, I'd bet on the mother."

This is not to say that mothers are perfect. Through all my research and interviewing, the trouble was, I was still too often impatient. I was still too often a poor listener, saying "uh-huh" when busy, not making eye contact and not really paying attention. Of course, my children knew it immediately. One day as I was typing away, Greg came in, asked how the book was going, and then commented, "When people write books like this, people think the mother is perfect but, really, behind the scenes, it's not like it sounds. It sounds like she must be fantastic but, in real life, she's just like every mom, she's an unperfect mom." This is surely the truth.

Although our day-to-day actions are unquestionably flawed, most mothers have a positive and strongly loving attitude toward their children. This attitude is carried with a child for life, long after tutoring and educational intervention are forgotten. When I interviewed successful learning-disabled children, they told me over and over again that one parent—sometimes a mother, sometimes a father—played a pivotal role in their lives. I believe my father did this for me. "You can write, you're a good writer," he would tell me. My teachers never gave me great grades, but that did not affect him a bit. He'd continue to sing my praises. After receiving a job at a large publishing house, I remember him telling me, "You should write a book." "Dad, I'm living in New York City," I told him. "You don't know the competition." Just as he ignored my grades, he ignored my hesitancy, countering, "No, it will be great. I can see it."

His words of encouragement still ring in my ears. When the first rejection letters came in, it was, I believe, his total confidence that gave me the courage to continue. More than anything, this is the spirit I want to convey to my sons.

A leading New York City psychologist who has worked with learning-disabled children for more than thirty years, found that successful children were not necessarily those with the fewest problems, nor even those with the greatest intelligence; they were the ones who had one parent with unswerving faith in them. When asked how they were able to overcome their problems and succeed, they were the children who recalled:

- "My mother always thought I was the most wonderful child. . . ."
- "My mother, deep down, truly felt I was fabulous."
- "My mother always believed in me."

It is our unspoken messages that our children carry into their future. Our faith becomes theirs; our humor shows them the brighter side. For every child, there should be, deep in his heart, a mother cheering from the wings.

We can be their backers, but we must, in the end, separate. It is their values, their goals, their lives. We can only hope our extra emotional support will help them achieve the dreams they hold for themselves.

APPENDIX A

Practical Tips for Mothers

Many books have long reading lists. They always make me feel guilty—just more things I should do and probably never will. So instead, I decided to include what I always needed: practical, easy-to-do tips from mothers.

Play Catch with the Numbers by Throwing Them (All but Number 6) to Your Mitt. This trick came to my mind when I was desperate for a solution to my son's constant reversals. He just could not remember which way the numbers were written. He has a passion for baseball, so I told him to throw all the numbers toward his mitt (left hand)—except for number 6 (1, 2, 3, 4, 5, 7, 8, 9). He was six at the time, so I told him number 6 had to go the other way—a home run on its way out of the ballpark. This is how he learned to write his numbers properly. It was a real breakthrough, and it made me ecstatic.

For Organization: Buy Stacked Drawers in the Hardware Store and Label with Each Subject. One mother told me the best thing she did for her disorganized son was to buy eight plastic drawers in the hardware store. She piled one on top of another and labeled each drawer with a course name. He put all his papers and assignments for each subject in the appropriate drawer. For the first time, he was able to keep things straight. At the end of the semester, he emptied the drawers and started over. He is now a high school senior, and he still uses these drawers. She said they will be packed up for college, too.

Use House Steps for Teaching Early Math. "This is the only way our son could see what we were doing," one mother told me. It was concrete and it worked.

Give a Time Warning. Say "In fifteen minutes I am going to ask you to begin your homework," or whatever. Such advance notice helps with time management. One mother said a therapist had recommended it, and it really helped.

Wear Your Watch on Your Left Arm. This is my son's suggestion for a quick way to remember right and left. He explained he always wears his watch on his left arm, so if someone says "Put your right hand up," he can do it *fast*.

Buy Solid-Color Sheets and Quilts. For the child already overloaded with stimuli, solids (some say pastels are better than primary colors) have a calming effect. Walls, curtains, and rugs should be a solid color too.

Get a Tetherball Set. While some children have trouble catching or hitting a ball, they all love tetherball; it's fun for any athletic ability. Sets cost under twenty dollars and take up little room. The children do kill the grass around them, but look on the positive side: they are not gathered around the open refrigerator door or leaving wet glass rings on your table!

Use an Egg Timer to Pace Homework. My son would begin his homework and then get up to have a snack, then make a phone call, and so on. A teacher told me to have him set an egg timer for fifteen minutes and gradually extend the periods. He had to work that long before a break. It was very simple but worked well.

Take a Sketch Pad and Pencils Along to the Museum. I found sketching focused and involved the children: They liked selecting what to sketch, and it helped them to remember things. A pad is better than loose paper. They enjoyed colored pencils, too. For older children, the audio guides, which are a bit like treasure hunts, are better than just browsing.

Get a Three-Hole Punch That Fits Right into Their Three-Ring Binder. This was a school suggestion, and it really worked well.

Let Them Make Lunch. One mother has her daughter make her own lunch each day. She prepares it while her mom is making dinner. It builds independence, and you won't hear those familiar refrains, "Gosh, Mom, what did you put in that sandwich? It was awful!"

Get an Extra Set of Home Textbooks. We all know the problem: it is 9 P.M., your child is about to begin his history homework, only to discover he inadvertently left the textbook in his locker. One mother's solution: ask the school, at the beginning of the year, for an extra set of home textbooks.

Take Day Trips. These children learn through experience: abstractions can be difficult. Years ago, my son came home from school and excitedly told me he had to pick one state from the United States for a term report. He picked France; he hoped he got it because three other kids had picked it, too! Visiting real historical places is concrete and understandable. Reading the map is a great way to learn direction, an often confusing concept.

Seek Excellent Drivers Education. Many mothers told me their children had trouble learning to drive (a perceptually complex task), so individual instruction may be more successful than an in-school program. Right-left confusion can also make driving difficult. Tell the student to be certain he is sitting on or near the road's center line.

Hide the House Key. Believe it or not, this took me time to figure out. I carried my key; I figured they would do the same. But, invariably, they misplaced or forgot it. By hiding it near the house, it's always handy.

Use Graph Paper for Math. One boy's calculations used to be crunched up in the corner of his paper. His father, who is from Italy, learned math on graph paper. So, he bought his son graph paper, which helped him space his tabulations. Once he could see the work clearly, math became his strongest subject.

Turn the Ruled Notebook Paper Horizontally, to Create Columns for Math. This is a wonderfully ingenious trick devised by one mother to help her son keep his math columns straight. She said it avoided the embarrassment of his using different paper than the other children.

Buy "Fat" Pencils and Pens. They are much easier to hold and manipulate.

Give Your Child a Camera. Taking pictures focuses your child and makes him an active, rather than passive, participant. Children can start taking pictures at a young age (be prepared for pictures of cutoff heads) and get more sophisticated in skill as they get older.

Get "No Bounce" Check-Writing Privileges. Every mother I interviewed who had a child older than eighteen said, "Oh, the bounced checks!" Services that prevent bounced checks should be established when you open a checking account.

Collect Soda Cans. Collecting and refunding soda cans can be done by children of all ages. They can earn money for their purchases and practice money skills. In our school, the children collected cans and then donated the proceeds to a charity for the homeless.

Put a Month-by-Month, Three-Hole Punched Calendar in the Looseleaf Notebook. Learning-disabled students are prone to what my younger son calls the *P* word—procrastination. Calendars come notebook-ready and are terrific for remembering test dates and planning term papers.

Stress Organization. "The main thing these children need, more than anything, is organization," a learning specialist told me. "From day one, this is what a mother must stress—from laying out their clothes the night before, to a bunch of sharpened pencils on their desk, to a study area separate from their play space, to fixed wake-up and bedtime."

A Trick for the Multiplication Table. This is one both my children rely on. I find it confusing, but since they find it great—here goes: when multiplying any number by 9 (for example, 5), subtract 1 from what you are multiplying by (making it *4*), then count up to 9 (5, 6, 7, 8, 9 = 5 things), so, 9 × 5 = 45.

Buy Stories on Tape. Most bookstores sell great literature on tape. One mother said her son listens while playing Legos, making models, or whenever he's home sick. She also keeps a few in the car for long drives. The Agatha Christie mysteries, *Ivanhoe,* and *Huckleberry Finn* are particular favorites. Cassette players and tapes are provided free, through the Library of Congress for those who qualify through their local committee on the handicapped. For academic work as well as pleasure, free tapes are also available through Recordings for the Blind.

Color Code Notebooks and Books. Have a green book jacket and a green notebook for English, for example. It reduces locker panic and helps organization.

Get a Magazine Subscription. My son loved receiving something with his name on it in the mail. While he rarely read for pleasure, he sat down and read the articles in *Sports Illustrated* right away.

Read Out Loud. Some students who have trouble following directions or understanding what they read find that reading aloud helps. One father mentioned he was about to yell at his son for being on the phone when he realized he was reading his English lesson aloud!

Put a White Index Card Beneath the Line You Are Reading. For decoding difficulties, blocking out the lines below lessens distractions and keeps the reader on track.

Play Classical Music While Studying. Language processing goes on in the left hemisphere of your brain, with some input from the right hemisphere. Music is processed in your right hemisphere. By occupying the right hemisphere with music, you allow the left hemisphere to process language without wandering. The music must be without lyrics (no rock or opera); lyrics interrupt processing in the left hemisphere.

Don't Study in the Library. Several dyslexic students mentioned they had great difficulty concentrating in the library. One found the humming of fluorescent lights made her drowsy; another said the colors of all the books were distracting; still another commented that the people walking in and out and sitting down interrupted his thoughts and drove him crazy.

Use Standard Writing Formulas. At our son's special school, every book report began, "This book is about . . ." It was a formula, but it forced children to write a topic sentence. The following paragraphs always began, "Then. . . . Next. . . . Finally. . . ." It kept structure and order. Children eventually move beyond this standard, but I think such memorized formulas helped them.

Call School in August to Check on Teachers and Placement. It is wise to check *before* school begins. At that time, any necessary changes can be made more easily. Once school opens, the administration is very reluctant to make changes.

Alert Teachers to Possible Problems Before They Arise. One learning specialist advises alerting teachers to a child's needs at the start of the year. Often when problems arise it is too late and the teacher's attitude tends to be that the parent is just making an excuse.

Shop Late. Any supermarket that's open late will do. You can leave young children, especially hyperactive ones, home with your husband and avoid those supermarket scenes—those carts careening full-speed ahead, with your gleeful child at the helm. You'll also buy fewer sweet cereals!

Try Open Baskets for Toys and Limit the Number of Toys. Both suggestions make cleanup time easier and more effective.

Have Good Overhead Light Rather Than Many Lamps. Good overhead light creates an organized visual effect and prevents your child from sitting right next to the lamp, but never turning it on (we all know that scene!).

Get a Thesaurus. Stephen Sondheim, the brilliant Broadway lyricist, says it's his secret weapon. Using a thesaurus builds vocabulary, a common weakness, and prevents those constant cries "Mom, what's another word for . . ."

Make a List. One mother told me, "Whenever I went into my son's room, I was always yelling about the towels and clothes on the floor and nagging about the unmade bed. Exasperated, he shouted back, 'Make me a list!,' which is exactly what I do now. I tack it on his door and, believe it or not, it sometimes works!"

Convey "You Can Do It". A child cannot be teased or humiliated into academic success. Only with ease of mind is the door open for learning. My baseball-loving son told me, "Sometimes, when I go to bed, I say to myself, 'Let's go Mets.' It gives me courage; it gives me strength." While schoolwork is difficult for him, he definitely has that go-get-'em spirit about conquering it. Perhaps this is the secret. (When I told a psychiatrist friend about his method, she said, "You know, I'm going to try it!")

Hang in There. Things definitely do get better. With time and help, skills improve, interests emerge, and friendships develop. Many awkward six-year-olds turn into fabulous sixteen-year-olds and very successful twenty-six-year-olds!

APPENDIX B

Societies and Self-Help Groups

"The lifesaving advice," one mother said, "is finding other mothers in the same situation and joining a mothers' group. No one can fully understand but a mother who has been through it." This mother explained that when her group first met, there was a great deal of high-pitched, nervous laughter. After a few months, it totally disappeared, as the women relaxed and experienced real sharing.

Dyslexia societies sponsor support groups and much more. For example, the National Center for Learning Disabilities publishes *Their World,* an informative and inspiring magazine. The Orton Dyslexia Society offers outstanding conferences and workshops for both parents and professionals. Whenever I attended, I came home with renewed enthusiasm and great new ideas.

Large national societies have branches in many states. For the chapter in your area, first contact the headquarters listed below. Meetings are often listed in local newspapers as well.

Association for Children and
    Adults with Learning
    Disabilities
4156 Library Road
Pittsburgh, PA 15234
(412) 341-1515

Closer Look
1201 16th Street, N.W.
Washington, DC 20036
(202) 822-7900

Council for Exceptional Children
1920 Association Drive
Reston, VA 22091
(703) 620-3660

Federation for Children with
  Special Needs
312 Stuart Street, Second Floor
Boston, MA 02116
(617) 482-2915

Marin Puzzle People, Inc.
1368 Lincoln Avenue, Suite 105
San Rafael, CA 94901
(415) 453-4006

National Association for the
  Education of Young Children
1834 Connecticut Avenue, N.W.
Washington, DC 20009
(202) 232-8777

National Center for Learning
  Disabilities
99 Park Avenue
New York, NY 10016
(212) 687-7211
(formerly Foundation for
  Children with Learning
  Disabilities)

National Network of Learning
  Disabled Adults
808 N. 82d Street, Suite F2
Scottsdale, AZ 85257
(602) 941-5112

Orton Dyslexia Society Inc.
724 York Road
Baltimore, MD 21204
(301) 296-0232

Index

About the Author

ELIZABETH WEISS has written numerous books on women's health issues, including *The Anger Trap, Recovering from the Heart Attack Experience, From Female Depression to Contented Womanhood, Female Fatigue,* and *The Female Breast.* She is a frequent contributor to women's magazines and has appeared on many talk shows discussing these issues. A graduate of Skidmore College with a master's degree from Boston University, she lives with her husband, a physician, and two sons in New York City.